✫✫✫✫✫✫✫✫✫✫✫✫✫✫✫✫

BASEBALL
SUPERSTARS

Jackie Robinson

✫✫✫✫✫✫✫✫✫✫✫✫✫✫✫✫

✶✶✶✶✶✶✶✶✶✶✶✶✶✶✶✶

Hank Aaron
Ty Cobb
Lou Gehrig
Derek Jeter
Randy Johnson
Mike Piazza
Kirby Puckett
Jackie Robinson
Ichiro Suzuki
Bernie Williams

✶✶✶✶✶✶✶✶✶✶✶✶✶✶✶✶

BASEBALL SUPERSTARS

Jackie Robinson

Susan Muaddi Darraj

CHELSEA HOUSE
PUBLISHERS
An imprint of Infobase Publishing

JACKIE ROBINSON

Chelsea House
An imprint of Infobase Publishing
132 West 31st Street
New York NY 10001

Library of Congress Cataloging-in-Publication Data
Darraj, Susan Muaddi.
  Jackie Robinson / Susan Muaddi Darraj.
    p. cm. — (Baseball superstars)
  Includes bibliographical references and index.
  ISBN-13: 978-0-7910-9442-6 (hardcover)
  ISBN-10: 0-7910-9442-1 (hardcover)
  1. Robinson, Jackie, 1919-1972. 2. Baseball players—United States—Biography.
 3. African American baseball players—Biography. I. Title. II. Series.
  GV865.R6D37 2007
  796.357092—dc22
  [B]   2007005923

Chelsea House books are available at special discounts when purchased in bulk quantities for businesses, associations, institutions, or sales promotions. Please call our Special Sales Department in New York at (212) 967-8800 or (800) 322-8755.

You can find Chelsea House on the World Wide Web at http://www.chelseahouse.com

Series design by Erik Lindstrom
Cover design by Ben Peterson

Printed in the United States of America

Bang EJB 10 9 8 7 6 5 4 3 2 1

This book is printed on acid-free paper.

All links and Web addresses were checked and verified to be correct at the time of publication. Because of the dynamic nature of the Web, some addresses and links may have changed since publication and may no longer be valid.

✦ ✦ ✦ ✦ ✦ ✦ ✦ ✦ ✦ ✦ ✦ ✦ ✦ ✦ ✦ ✦

CONTENTS

1	A Difficult Summer	1
2	The Budding Superstar	7
3	From College to the Military	17
4	To the Big Leagues	27
5	Making History	38
6	A Public Figure	51
7	Advancing the Race	66
8	The Last Game	78
9	Troubling Times	90
10	Coming Home	97
	Statistics	108
	Chronology	109
	Timeline	110
	Glossary	112
	Bibliography	114
	Further Reading	115
	Index	118

A Difficult Summer

During the summer of 1939, young Jackie Robinson played a lot of softball, not baseball. The 20-year-old college student was in the physical prime of his life, and he had honed his skills by playing several sports for Pasadena Junior College, from football to baseball to track. He had secured admission to the University of California, Los Angeles (UCLA), and planned to play on at least two of its teams in the fall. Until then, the long California summer days and evenings were spent playing softball. It was a productive way to ease his stress, worries, and sorrow.

One of his worries was his decision to attend UCLA. In fact, Robinson, who was already an athletic legend in the region, had set his hopes on bigger schools, like Stanford or the University of Southern California (USC). Stanford University did not accept black students, however, and it was not planning to make an exception—even for an athlete as talented as Jackie "Jack Rabbit" Robinson, as he was called because of his speed. USC was a possibility, because it did have black players on its teams, but Robinson had studied the situation sufficiently to realize, to his disappointment, that these were often "token players." They were, in other words, members of the team, but to avoid controversy, they were not regularly offered opportunities to play. Robinson's friend and fellow athlete Ray Bartlett said, "We all knew USC had the best athletic program and the best teams. . . . They were *the* team in almost every sport in Southern California. But we knew we would just sit on the bench over there."

And more than anything else, Jackie Robinson wanted to play.

Sports had provided him with a form of therapy when, that summer, his family suffered a tragedy: the death of his older brother Frank. On July 10, Frank was killed when his motorcycle collided with a car that was traveling the opposite direction and turned in front of him. Frank was thrown into the air and slammed into a parked car hard enough to dent it. A passenger riding with Frank suffered a few minor injuries, but Frank's skull was fractured, several major bones were broken, and major organs were damaged. A few hours after the accident, he died at the hospital, leaving behind his wife, Maxine, and their children.

A mild-mannered man who had been frustrated many times by racism and the obstacles it created, Frank Robinson had struggled to find work and support himself. In fact, until his death, he had lived in his mother's house with his young family. This arrangement was very difficult for him because he felt that he should be able to provide for his own family, rather than depend on his mother, who was not financially stable herself.

Despite his personal frustrations and lost ambitions, Frank served as a father figure to Jackie, who was eight years younger. Jackie later recalled that Frank "was always there to protect

☆ ☆ ☆ ☆ ☆ ☆

A SPORTING FAMILY

Jackie Robinson was not the only athletic member of his family. For much of his youth, he followed in the fleet footsteps of his brother, Mack Robinson, who was five years older than Jackie. Through Mack, who excelled at track and field, Jackie first saw the excitement of sports. "I remember going to track meets with him," Robinson recalled in Arnold Rampersad's biography, "and watching him run and listening to the crowd yell."

Mack Robinson set junior-college records in the 100-meter dash, the 200-meter dash, and the long jump while at Pasadena Junior College. He attended the University of Oregon, graduating in 1941. There, he won many titles in NCAA and Pacific Coast Conference track meets, and he is a member of the University of Oregon Hall of Fame.

His greatest sporting accomplishment came in the 1936 Summer Olympics, which were held in Berlin, Germany. He finished second in the 200-meter dash, only 0.4 seconds behind the winner, Jesse Owens. Owens ended up capturing four gold medals at the 1936 Games, in the 100- and 200-meter dashes, the long jump, and the 400-meter relay.

Mack Robinson, who continued to live in Pasadena, was known for leading the fight against street crime there. The Pasadena Robinson Memorial, commemorating both Mack and Jackie Robinson, was dedicated in 1997. Three years later, Mack Robinson died of complications from diabetes, kidney failure, and pneumonia.

me when I was in a scrap, even though I don't think he could knock down a fly." During Jackie's high school and junior-college games, Frank had cheered him on from the stands. He had also acted as an unofficial scout by attending the games of competing teams to report to Jackie on certain players. This information often helped Jackie to prepare to face those players in football, basketball, and baseball games, or track meets. Frank's loss was a tremendous blow to the Robinson family, and especially to Jackie, who had lost a brother, father, and friend all in one.

A REPUTATION FOR TROUBLE

Two months after Frank's death, on September 5, Jackie played a softball game at Brookside Park in Pasadena with childhood buddy Ray Bartlett and other friends. After the game, he drove his pals home in his car, an "aging Plymouth . . . with Ray Bartlett and other friends riding playfully on the running boards." As Jackie paused at an intersection, a car driven by a white man pulled up next to them. He looked at Jackie, Ray, and the others and called them racial slurs. A furious Bartlett reached out and hit the man in the face. The man got out of his car, ready to confront Jackie and his friends, but he hesitated. A crowd of about 40 to 50 young black people who had apparently witnessed the incident suddenly appeared, hovering around the two cars.

At that moment, an officer pulled up on his motorcycle and began to question the young people, suspecting them of harassing the white driver. He tried to arrest several of them, but they escaped the scene. Among those who fled was Bartlett. Desperate to catch someone, the officer whipped out his gun and pointed it at Jackie Robinson, who had been the only "suspect" not to run away. Robinson knew that, in the past, blacks had been attacked and even killed by prejudiced white officers without recrimination. "I found myself up against the side of my car," he said, "with a gun barrel pressed unsteadily into the pit of my stomach. I was scared to death."

Football was one of several sports Jackie Robinson played when he was enrolled at the University of California, Los Angeles (UCLA). The summer of 1939, just before he entered UCLA, was a difficult one for Robinson. One of his older brothers was killed in a car accident, and then Robinson was unjustly arrested.

Robinson was formally charged with "hindering traffic" and "resisting arrest." He spent the night in jail, where officers did not permit him a phone call (to which he was entitled). He pleaded not guilty to the charges, posted bail, and was released. He was determined to fight the charges because, as was clear to him and everyone else, the arrest was a sham; had he been white, he would never have been in the situation in the first place.

Robinson's arrest alarmed the new head football coach at UCLA, Edwin "Babe" Horrell. He had been counting on Robinson to play with the Bruins that fall. Through Horrell and other prominent people, a deal was arranged: Robinson would plead guilty and not serve jail time. Robinson was not aware of the arrangement. When the case came to trial on October 18, Robinson was absent. His original plea of "not guilty" was changed to "guilty" without his knowledge. Essentially, members of the Pasadena community who were Bruins fans knew that Robinson was key to UCLA's success during the football season, and that saved him.

Although he avoided jail time, Robinson was angry when he realized that a guilty plea had been entered for him. He had been planning to fight the charges, which he knew to be unjust and unfounded.

Later, Robinson would admit, "I got out of that trouble because I was an athlete." The larger issue, however, disturbed him more than anything else: Racism was prevalent in Pasadena, as it was everywhere else in the country. A white man had nonchalantly offended a group of young black people, but it was one of those young men who had been punished. Furthermore, while white people had helped him escape the injustice of a jail sentence, they had only intervened because of Robinson's athletic abilities. What about the other black people in the United States who languished in jails, unsaved because they lacked the ability to catch a football or steal a base?

The incident, as Robinson recalled, was "my first personal experience with bigotry of the meanest sort." He would never forget it.

The Budding
Superstar

In 1919, the American South was far from a friendly place for African Americans. Although the Civil War had ended decades earlier and President Abraham Lincoln's Emancipation Proclamation had legally freed slaves, African Americans were still not completely free. This was the era in which Jim Crow laws were in full effect, threatening the opportunities for African Americans to improve their lives and their sense of self-respect and dignity.

Cairo was a small town deep in south Georgia, just a few miles from the Florida state line. The region had been known before the Civil War as the "Black Belt," because of the dense concentration of the African-American population. In the early twentieth century, most of the residents in this area were former slaves or the children of former slaves, and most had been unable to rise above dire poverty. The region consisted of former plantations, which had been transformed into "share-cropping" lands. Former white slave owners still owned these plantations, but they rented them out in parcels to African-American families, who worked on the land and kept a portion of the profits.

Jerry Robinson, a young African American, worked on a farm in Cairo, Georgia, on land owned by James Madison Sasser, a white landowner. Robinson, who was illiterate and never had a formal education, had lived in the area his entire life and had always worked for the Sasser family; however, his intelligent, motivated wife, Mallie McGriff, wanted a better life. Her parents, who were former slaves, believed in the power of education. They owned the land on which they had raised their 14 children, and they pressed all of them to attend school. Mallie had completed the sixth grade, which as biographer Arnold Rampersad notes, was "no small feat for a black girl in rural Georgia." In fact, as a young girl, Mallie taught her own father how to read and write.

Mallie McGriff met Jerry Robinson in 1906, when he was 18 and she was only 14. Despite her parents' objections—they had higher hopes for their daughter—she continued to see Robinson over the next three years until they were married on November 21, 1909, when Mallie was 17 years old. They lived in a small cottage on the Sasser plantation, where Jerry worked while Mallie took care of their children. Their son Edgar was born in 1910, Frank in 1911, and Mack in 1914; finally they had a daughter, which Mallie had always wanted, in 1916, and she was named Willa Mae.

Mallie pushed and encouraged her husband to strive for better working conditions and better pay from Sasser. Robinson usually made only $12 a month, so Mallie insisted that Sasser give him sharecropper status, rather than just employee status.

JIM CROW

The era after the Civil War, from 1865 to 1876, brought many freedoms and rights to African Americans. Known as the Reconstruction, this period gave hope to many that equality between the races would soon become a reality. Reconstruction addressed the return of the Southern states that had seceded during the Civil War and the legal status of the freed African-American slaves. As civil rights increased, though, so did white reaction against them.

Beginning in 1876, many Southern states began to enact laws meant to separate the races, known as segregation. For example, laws were put into place that banned white nurses from tending to black patients or even working in a ward with black patients. Other states segregated hospital wards entirely, establishing white and black wards, while others designated separate hospitals altogether.

Other laws aimed to segregate the races in general society. Before long, most Southern states dictated that black people had to drink from separate water fountains, attend separate schools, eat at separate restaurants, and sit in the back of public buses. Of course, black institutions, such as black schools, were accorded less funding than white schools, and thus established a legacy of inequality and lack of opportunity. These laws that segregated public facilities became known as Jim Crow laws. The term comes from a minstrel-show song, "Jump Jim Crow."

In sports, segregation also applied: black and white athletes were prohibited from playing in the same games, so separate leagues or teams were usually developed for black players.

Sasser was not happy but agreed to the arrangement, which would mean that, rather than pay Robinson a monthly salary, Sasser would give him land, fertilizer, and supplies and then collect half of whatever Robinson earned.

In this way, Mallie was able to help her husband earn more money for their young family. They grew many types of crops, and they also raised several animals, like hogs, chickens, and turkeys, which brought in a nice profit. Life began to improve slowly, but Jerry Robinson's eyes began to turn toward other women. Before long, Mallie became aware that he was carrying on romances with other women as well as spending money while out on the town. He and Mallie fought increasingly, and they even separated a few times, but Mallie always forgave him and took him back.

So, when Mallie became pregnant again in 1918, she wondered if her marriage would survive the added strain of a fifth child. Jack Roosevelt Robinson was born on the evening of January 31, 1919, at the height of the Spanish flu epidemic, which killed millions of people around the world and in the United States in 1918 and 1919. His middle name, Roosevelt, was a testament to former President Teddy Roosevelt, who had died earlier that month, on January 6. (Roosevelt had been seen by many as progressive—at least, more progressive than most other political leaders—on the cause of African-American rights.) Jack, who quickly became nicknamed "Jackie," was a healthy, happy baby who became his mother's joy.

Jerry Robinson, however, became Mallie's heartache again. In July 1919, six months after Jackie's birth, Jerry told Mallie that he was taking a trip to Texas to visit relatives. He wanted Willa Mae to accompany him, but Mallie, suspicious of his intentions, would not allow her daughter to go. Jerry left and did not return for a long while, and Mallie knew that her qualms had been well-founded: He had abandoned her and the children.

Years later in his memoir, Jackie Robinson, who was an infant when his father left, wrote, "To this day I have no idea what became of my father. Later, when I became aware of how much my mother had to endure alone, I could only think of him with bitterness. He, too, may have been a victim of oppression, but he had no right to desert my mother and five children." Indeed, Jerry Robinson's desertion left Mallie in a terrible predicament: Without Jerry to work on the farm, they could not live up to their sharecropping agreement with Sasser. Mallie tried to take several different jobs, but she could not earn enough money; soon, Sasser evicted her and the five children from his property. In a way, the eviction forced Mallie to make a decision: The South, especially Georgia, would never be a welcome place to raise her children.

In the months after Jackie's birth, a number of violent, anti-black acts occurred: in April, two white policemen were killed in eastern Georgia and, in retaliation, five African Americans were murdered and seven black churches were burned to the ground. A race riot erupted in May in Charleston, South Carolina. The violence continued during what came to be known as the "Red Summer" until September, when an epidemic of arson struck many black churches and schools across Georgia.

Mallie's half-brother lived in California with his family; the American West was an unknown territory to Mallie, who had lived in the South her entire life. But, she reasoned, it had to be better than Georgia, which had a reputation as the most virulently racist state in an already racist region.

Thus, when Jerry Robinson eventually did return to Mallie several months later, asking her to take him back, it was too late. In May 1920, when Jackie was just 16 months old, Mallie packed up her family and boarded a train out of Georgia, heading toward the opposite end of the United States.

GROWING UP IN PASADENA

Several members of Mallie's family accompanied her to California: her sister, Cora Wade, and her husband and children, and their brother, Paul McGriff. Together, they arrived in Los Angeles in June 1920, hoping for a better life for their children than the Deep South would offer. They lived in an apartment in nearby Pasadena, cramped but happy, with Mallie's half-brother.

Mallie quickly found work as a maid for a white family who respected her and offered her a working schedule that suited her. The schedule enabled her to be home with her children in the evenings and to supervise them closely. She instilled in all of her children a sense of family loyalty and responsibility and a love of God and the church. She also encouraged them to respect themselves and to be generous and charitable to others.

Financially, however, times were difficult: Mallie often resorted to welfare relief to supplement her salary. Jackie Robinson wrote in his memoir that "sometimes there were only two meals a day, and some days we wouldn't have eaten at all if it hadn't been for the leftovers my mother was able to bring home from her job. There were other times when we subsisted on bread and sweet water." Nevertheless, Mallie budgeted carefully and was able to save money over time.

Within two years, Mallie and Cora's husband had earned enough money to buy a home for the two families, at 121 Pepper Street, in an all-white neighborhood. Eventually, the Wades bought a home of their own, making Mallie the sole owner of the house. Living in an all-white neighborhood came with its problems: Like the rest of the United States, Pasadena, California, had its share of racist and prejudiced citizens. At the time, only slightly more than 1,000 African Americans lived in

Mallie Robinson posed for a family portrait around 1925, when she and her children were living in Pasadena, California. With her were her five children: *(from left)* Mack, Jackie, Edgar, Willa Mae, and Frank. When Jackie was a young boy, with his mother working long days, Willa Mae became a surrogate to her little brother.

Pasadena (population 45,000), which was generally an affluent town. Restaurants, theaters, and other public establishments tried to bar African Americans, while job discrimination led the majority of African Americans to be employed only in low-paying jobs. White people in Pasadena, for the most part, did not want African Americans living in their neighborhoods.

Willa Mae Robinson, Jackie's sister, later said of those difficult first years on Pepper Street, "We went through a sort of slavery, with the whites slowly, very slowly, getting used to us." Someone burned a cross on their lawn, while others wanted to buy them out to force them to move; neighbors frequently called the police to complain that Mallie's children were noisy and disruptive. Her Christian spirit made her refuse to retaliate, and she suffered the abuse patiently, showing her neighbors only respect. Over the years, that sense of restraint and charity would help bridge the gap of mistrust and hatred and gain the Robinsons acceptance among their neighbors.

Mallie worked long days and could not be home with Jackie, who was still too young to attend school with his siblings. Willa Mae, his older sister, became a surrogate mother to Jackie, taking him to school with her every day so that their mother could go to work. Jackie played outside in the schoolyard sandbox while his sister watched him through her classroom's window. Occasionally, the teachers would bring him snacks and help supervise him as well. Willa Mae also took care of Jackie when they returned home from school every day, playing with him and feeding him until their mother came home. "I have few early school memories after graduating from the sandbox, but I do remember being aware of the constant protective attitude of my sister," Robinson recalled in his autobiography.

When Jackie was old enough to attend school, he proved to be a hard-working and dedicated student. However, he also experienced racial prejudice very early, and it upset him a great deal. Once, when he was eight years old, a girl who lived across the street taunted him and called him a racial slur several times as he stood sweeping the sidewalk in front of his house. Outraged, he shouted back at her, calling her a derogatory term, which angered the girl's father, who threatened to beat up Jackie. They ended up throwing stones at each other across the street until the girl's mother made her husband give up and come back inside. Jackie's fighting spirit would be remarked upon later in his career as well.

As an adolescent, he began to hang out with the Pepper Street Gang, a group of African-, Japanese-, and Mexican-American children who came from poor families. They committed minor crimes, like stealing fruit from produce sellers or throwing clumps of dirt at passing cars. Mallie worried that her son would fall into a bad habit of misbehavior, which could lead to trouble as an adult. She encouraged him to become more involved in the church.

A SPORTS MECCA

Jackie Robinson was lucky, in many ways, to grow up in Pasadena, not just because it offered a better life than Georgia (despite the prevalence of racism), but also because Pasadena was heavily invested in sports. Pasadena residents were sports lovers who followed high school and college teams, as well as professional games, closely. They had well-developed athletic programs in their communities and schools.

As a child, Jackie demonstrated an early talent for athletics. "In grammar school," he wrote, "some of my classmates would share their lunches with me if I played on their team." When Jackie attended Washington Junior High School, he joined the baseball and football teams, and he excelled at both sports. When he moved on to John Muir Technical High School, he also did well, largely because "by 1935 Muir Tech had developed an outstanding regional reputation as a sports powerhouse," according to Rampersad.

At Muir, Jackie stretched his abilities and tried basketball and track as well. He stunned his coaches by performing superbly in every sport he played, and he quickly became a legend in the area. He would begin the school year in one sport, then switch to the next as soon as the season had ended; he earned letters in all four sports. Local newspapers, which followed high school sports closely, described him as the "mainstay" of his team and "the nucleus of his squad."

Jackie's competitive spirit was driven by several factors, mainly his mother's wish for him and his siblings to improve their lives. Friend Ray Bartlett once described Jackie's competitive nature:

> He was a hard loser. By that I mean he always played his best and did his best and gave all he had, and he didn't like to lose. He liked to be the best, and he would be unhappy at school the day after we lost. He took losses very hard. The rest of us might shrug off a loss, but Jack would cry if we lost.

His intensity was reflected in his playing technique, which was smart and focused. During a basketball game for the Muir Terriers in January 1937, Jackie dominated the court. A local newspaper praised him: "Robinson was all over the floor . . . and when he wasn't scoring points he was making impossible 'saves' and interceptions, and was the best player on the floor." Other newspapers often featured stories with laudatory comments on his performances in games and tournaments.

As his reputation as a local sports superstar grew, Jackie became less involved in the Pepper Street Gang and its delinquent activities. In the little spare time he had, he became more and more active with the church instead, much to his mother's relief.

From College to the Military

On February 1, 1937, Jackie Robinson enrolled at Pasadena Junior College, which would be an important place in his sports career. Although he was one of only 70 African-American students at the college, Pasadena Junior College offered its minority students a status equal to that of their white peers. For the most part, Jim Crow laws did not apply on the Pasadena campus, where facilities and events were open to all students regardless of race.

Jackie followed his brother Mack to Pasadena Junior College; Mack had already earned a national reputation as a premier track star. In 1936, he made the United States Olympic team and finished second to Jesse Owens in the 200-meter dash at the Summer Olympics in Berlin, Germany. Despite his stardom, Mack encountered racism everywhere he went, which was a lesson for his younger brother, who understood that his reputation as an athlete could only take him so far.

Jackie starred in four sports for the Pasadena Junior College Bulldogs—baseball, football, basketball, and track—and he became an asset to every team. One day in his second year at the school, he made history in two sports on the same day: In the morning, he set a national junior-college record in the broad jump, and in the afternoon, he played in a baseball game that won his team the championship.

Although he was a versatile athlete, Jackie seemed to enjoy baseball the most. He especially became known for his quick baserunning and his ability to steal bases daringly. (He teased the pitchers and drove spectators into a frenzy by stealing home base on many occasions, prompting one reporter to say, "That isn't stealing . . . It's grand larceny.") Playing shortstop, he was a tremendous contributor to a successful baseball season for the junior college. In one game against Modesto Junior College, he got onto first base, then successively stole second, third, and home to score a run for the Bulldogs.

Jackie's family encouraged him and showed its pride in his athletic achievements. One person who was constantly in his corner was his brother Frank, who attended all his games. "I wanted to win," Jackie recalled years later, "not only for myself but also because I didn't want to see Frank disappointed." When Jackie set the broad-jump record, beating the mark held by his brother Mack, Mack was proud of Jackie's achievement, rather than jealous.

Jackie also attracted excitement on the football field, where he proved to be a quick runner and an excellent strategist. Reporters commented on his ability to make and receive passes with astonishing accuracy as well as outmaneuver opposing players to score touchdowns. "With such inspired playing," writes Rampersad, "Jack ended the [football] season a hero to the student body and to much of Pasadena." Discrimination, though, was still at play, as the Most Valuable Player award that

Jackie Robinson, playing for the University of California, Los Angeles, is shown running back a 63-yard punt return in a 1939 game against the University of Washington. Robinson had been a four-sport star at Pasadena Junior College, and he would go on to letter in four sports at UCLA.

year was given to someone else. When the team traveled to play other schools, Jack and his African-American teammates were frequently refused service at restaurants with the rest of the team and were denied hotel rooms in many cities.

Jackie, however, was not willing to put up with discrimination. During a basketball game at Long Beach Junior College, an opposing player blatantly punched Jackie, who fought back and easily beat him. The spectators erupted in anger, sparking a near-riot. He earned a reputation for having a bad temper, although many critics did not consider that he often had to deal with offensive comments and barbs from opponents on the field or the court.

THE REVEREND DOWNS

Despite his status in Pasadena as a sports hero, Jackie continued to have occasional run-ins with the local authorities, which gained him some notoriety—perhaps unfairly—as a troublemaker. In January 1938, he was arrested when he and a friend, driving home from a movie, began to sing a song called "Flat Foot Floogie." A policeman overheard them, thought they were insulting him, and decided to confront the two young men. Jackie spent the night in jail. At his sentencing, the judge gave him 10 days in jail but then allowed him to avoid serving the term as long as he stayed out of trouble for the next two years. He was now officially on probation, and he was keenly aware that his athletic ability was all that kept him out of jail.

The Reverend Karl Downs, a young pastor, moved to the Pasadena area that January to minister to the African-American community at the Scott United Methodist Church. Before long, his youth, zeal, and energy helped to bring more and more young people like Jackie Robinson back to the church. Downs had heard about Jackie and was determined to win him over; he acted like a friend and made himself available to talk and listen to Jackie's problems. "One of the frustrations of my teens was watching Mother work so hard," Robinson wrote in his memoir. "I wanted to help more, but I knew how much my college education meant to her. . . . When I talked to Karl about this and other problems, he helped ease some of my tensions. It wasn't so much what he did to help as the fact that he was interested and concerned enough to offer the best advice he could." Jackie credits Downs with being one of the people who rescued him during a troubling period of his life, when he—more likely than not—would have headed down a wrong path.

Instead, Jackie adopted a disciplined life and developed respect for himself and others. Unlike his peers, he refused to drink alcohol or date women he did not care about; this seeming contradiction between his local celebrity and his austere lifestyle puzzled many of his friends and teammates.

As Jackie was completing his two years at Pasadena Junior College, several local universities expressed an interest in him, knowing that he would be a tremendous asset to their athletic programs. Other schools, though, like Stanford University, would not accept him because he was African American. In the end, he decided to enroll at UCLA, which had a formidable sports program.

The death of his brother Frank in a car accident occurred shortly after he accepted the UCLA scholarship. Frank's death took a severe toll on Jackie, who buried his sorrows by playing more intensely than ever. At UCLA, he became the university's first athlete to letter in four sports, and he rapidly became a campus celebrity. Eventually, he focused on football and baseball only. In his spare time, he taught Sunday school at the Scott United Methodist Church, at the Reverend Downs's request.

One day, his friends introduced him to a pretty student on campus named Rachel Isum. They quickly fell in love and had a very deep, special relationship that included honesty. "I respected the fact that she never hesitated to disagree with my point of view," Jackie later recalled. Rachel was also a dedicated and hard-working student who came from a large and warm family.

Despite his athletic success at UCLA, however, Jackie decided to drop out in 1941, before completing his degree. "I was convinced that no amount of education would help a black man get a job," Robinson wrote in his memoir about his decision. He wanted to help his mother financially, which meant getting a job that could pay the bills, although many

Jackie Robinson heads off to practice at **UCLA**. His sports success made him a campus celebrity, but he decided to leave college after two years. "I was convinced that no amount of education would help a black man get a job," Robinson wrote in his memoir about that era.

people—Rachel, the Reverend Downs, and Mallie Robinson herself—tried to persuade him to stay in school.

MILITARY SERVICE

Jackie Robinson worked for the National Youth Association for some time, directing its athletic program. The National Youth Association provided jobs, job training, and relief to people ages 16 to 25. Later he worked at other jobs and played in semiprofessional football games for extra money. In March 1942, just a few months after the bombing of Pearl Harbor and the United States' entrance into World War II, Robinson was drafted by the U.S. military. During his service in the Army, he maintained contact with Rachel Isum through long letters, which he wrote and received at a regular rate. By this point, he was seriously envisioning himself married to her someday.

In the Army, despite performing his responsibilities dutifully, he experienced—and resisted—discrimination on many levels. At Fort Riley in Kansas, where he reported for basic training, he was barred from playing on the baseball team. The officer who led the team had told others that he would break the team up before a black man would play on it. A year later, he was denied again, being told that "you have to play with the colored team." There was no team for the African-American players, though, so he was effectively being told to go away.

He was invited, however, to play on the football team. Happy for the opportunity, Robinson played exceptionally well during practices and proved to be an invaluable team member. It became clear, though, before the first game, scheduled with the University of Missouri, that the opponents would refuse to play a team that had a black member. Rather than tell him the truth, the Army gave him leave to return home for a short while. When he returned, he was adamant: "I said that I had no intention of playing football for a team which, because I was black, would not allow me to play all the games." The colonel reminded Robinson that he could be ordered to play; Robinson replied, "You wouldn't want me playing on your team, knowing that my heart wasn't in it," and the matter was dropped.

Another time, after he had been designated an officer, his men complained that only a few seats were assigned for

★ ★ ★ ★ ★

BLACK TROOPS DURING WORLD WAR II

On December 7, 1941, the Japanese air force bombed the U.S. naval base at Pearl Harbor, Hawaii, triggering America's entrance into World War II. Jackie Robinson joined the U.S. Army in 1942, when he was 23 years old.

The draft had been put into place in 1940, and about 2.5 million African-American men registered for it. One million were actually called to serve, most of them in the Army. Furthermore, many African-American women also volunteered to serve in the military, usually as nurses. The paradox of fighting a war for the United States was not lost on these young men and women—they understood that they were defending a country that had yet to fulfill its promise of equality to them.

Even while serving, the African-American troops had to endure indignities and injustice, such as inferior lodgings for their regiments. The units were just as segregated as American society at the time, so the African-American soldiers found that even their loyalty to their country was marred by the race barrier. The African-American nurses encountered race-based conflicts as well, such as when wounded white soldiers did not want black nurses tending to them.

African-American soldiers in the post exchange, where many soldiers went to relax and eat. When Robinson called a superior officer to ask if this rule could be changed, the superior, not knowing Robinson's race, bluntly said, "Lieutenant, let me put it to you this way. How would you like to have your wife sitting next to [an African American]?" Furious, Robinson began to shout at the officer, and the conversation became very heated. The colonel of their unit became involved and resolved the dispute; in the end, though the seating sections remained segregated, more seats were allowed for African-American soldiers.

A more serious racial incident occurred on July 6, 1943. Robinson had used the Army transportation bus to ride to the hospital, where he was staying as a patient (his ankle had been bothering him for many months). During the ride, he saw the wife of one of his lieutenants and sat with her, chatting. The bus driver, thinking the woman was white (she was not), ordered Robinson to sit at the back of the bus.

Across the country, Jim Crow laws had ensured that all aspects of American life were segregated, including seating on buses. Robinson, however, knew that the Army had banned racial discrimination on its vehicles because of recent scandals involving legendary boxer Joe Louis, who had refused to move to the back of an Army bus. Robinson ignored the bus driver's commands. The driver grew more irate and started to scream at Robinson, who yelled back that he knew his rights and he would not move to the back of the bus. When the bus arrived at its destination, the driver reported Robinson, who was questioned and then taken into custody.

"I was naïve about the elaborate lengths to which racists in the Armed Forces would go to put a vocal black man in his place," Robinson later wrote of the incident. He was informed by a white officer who was friendly to him that he might be framed, as rumors had circulated that a black lieutenant had gotten drunk and started trouble on a bus. Robinson took a blood test, which proved that he had not been drinking.

The African-American media wrote about the situation in detail, portraying the Army as a racist institution. Later, when Robinson faced a court-martial on charges of misbehaving and being drunk, he was acquitted on all charges. Robinson was honorably discharged from the military in November 1944.

4

To the
Big Leagues

While in the military, Jackie Robinson asked Rachel Isum to marry him, and she agreed. They had several difficult times, even breaking up at one point for several months when Isum joined the Nurse Cadet Corps, but they reunited and eagerly began to make wedding plans.

Now that he was out of the Army, Robinson needed a job. The Reverend Karl Downs, who had become president of Samuel Houston College in Austin, Texas, offered him the position of physical education teacher at the college. Robinson moved there by Christmas of 1944.

A month earlier, he had met Ted Alexander, a soldier stationed at Camp Breckinridge in Kentucky, who had played baseball for the Kansas City Monarchs, part of the Negro American League. Alexander suggested that Robinson try out for the Monarchs, who needed talent since many black baseball players had been sent to fight in the war. The Monarchs offered Robinson $400 if he could make the team, and they invited him to attend tryouts in Houston, Texas, in April.

The Negro Leagues came about in the years after a decision in 1868 by the National Association of Baseball Players to ban any ball club that included African-American players from joining the association. In 1885, as African-American players were excluded from teams that wanted to become professional, the first all-black baseball team, the Cuban Giants, was established.

In 1920, Rube Foster founded an all-black baseball league, the Negro National League. Other leagues popped up, but after a few years, the two leagues that became the most prominent were a new Negro National League, founded in 1933, and the Negro American League, founded in 1937. These leagues operated quite successfully, although they enjoyed little of the fame that the professional, all-white leagues did—not to mention the salaries. Many black stars, however—including Satchel Paige and Josh Gibson—made their careers in these leagues and young African-American sportsmen hoped to join them.

Until April, Robinson worked diligently as the physical education teacher at Samuel Houston College. He was proud that the Reverend Downs, whom he deeply respected, had offered him the position, and he wanted to do a solid job. The college, which was founded by the United Methodist Church as an institution of higher learning for African Americans, was in financial trouble, but Downs, with his energy and spirit, was changing those circumstances. Bringing Jackie Robinson to campus was part of Downs's plan to inspire the students to take pride in the college. Robinson suited the job perfectly; he displayed his awards and trophies to serve as an inspiration to the students, and he set about building an athletic program almost from scratch, given free rein by Downs.

In 1945, Jackie Robinson began to play for the Kansas City Monarchs of the Negro American League. Robinson did not like the long road trips on uncomfortable buses and the constant night games that came with playing in the Negro Leagues.

In April 1945, as planned, he traveled to Houston to try out for the Monarchs. He easily made the team but was shocked to discover the lack of professionalism that plagued the leagues in many ways. "Spring training," he realized, "consisted of actually playing baseball games rather than getting prepared for the coming season." He realized that the league directors and team owners just wanted to use the players to make as much money as possible. Although the Monarchs were one of the best-treated teams in the Negro Leagues, the team members still had to deal with inferior treatment when traveling—they were not permitted to eat in certain restaurants, and they had to stay in subpar hotels designated for African Americans. Also, the owners would make the teams play as often as possible, since the games attracted many spectators and generated business.

In his memoir, Robinson described one particularly bad road trip:

> On one occasion, we left Kansas City on a bus on a Sunday night, traveled to Philadelphia, reaching there Tuesday morning. We played a doubleheader that night, and the next day we were on the road again. This fatiguing travel wouldn't have been so bad if we could have had decent meals. Finding satisfactory or even passable eating places was almost a daily problem.

OPPORTUNITY DENIED

Robinson did not hide his unhappiness with the Negro American League very well. He later wrote, "All the time I was playing, I was looking around for something else. I didn't like the bouncing buses, the cheap hotels, and the constant night games." Being a member of the Monarchs, however, did call more attention to his talent. For example, in April 1945, he and two other Negro League players were sent to Boston to try out for the Red Sox. Politics in Boston helped lead to the try-out—a city councilman wanted to draw attention to the racial discrimination that existed in professional baseball. Though Robinson did not really think that he or the others would make the team, the opportunity was exciting. Indeed, Robinson did make an impression on the Boston Red Sox players and coaches, but race issues once again obstructed advancement. "What a ballplayer!" the chief scout for the Red Sox was overheard saying about Robinson. Then he added, "Too bad he's the wrong color."

At the time, biographer Arnold Rampersad explains, there was no formal ban in professional baseball against allowing African Americans to play. In 1942, the baseball commissioner, Kenesaw Mountain Landis, stated clearly that "Negroes are not barred from organized baseball" by his office. Year after year, however, no African-American players debuted on any major-league teams. Team owners did not want to be the first to break the color barrier, and park owners were happy with the situation, since they rented their stadiums to the Negro League squads when they were not being used by the major-league teams.

A small movement within professional baseball—consisting of sports journalists, team owners, and even some players—was trying to contest the status quo. It was Jackie Robinson's good fortune—or perhaps *baseball's* good fortune—that his career intersected with the rise of this movement to integrate professional baseball.

THE STEPS TOWARD INTEGRATION

Unbeknownst to Robinson, Branch Rickey had been quietly working in his own way to integrate professional baseball. The general manager of the Brooklyn Dodgers, Rickey was a devout Christian who idolized leaders who made daring moves, such as Abraham Lincoln (indeed, a portrait of Lincoln hung in his office).

Ever since he was a young man, he had been haunted by an experience that had offered him a glimpse of the travesty of racial hatred. In 1904, Rickey was the coach of the Ohio Wesleyan University ball club. His team had traveled to South Bend, Indiana, to play Notre Dame. Charles Thomas, the team's only African-American player, was barred from the hotel where the team was staying. Appalled, Rickey negotiated with the hotel manager to allow Thomas to stay with the rest of the team; in the end, the issue was resolved by the manager's insistence that Thomas could share a room with Rickey himself, to which Rickey agreed. Thomas—humiliated and frustrated—shocked his coach later, when he began to scratch his hands, saying, "Damned skin . . . damned skin! If only I could rub it off."

★ ★ ★ ★ ★

BRANCH RICKEY

The man whom Jackie Robinson once referred to as his father figure was born Wesley Branch Rickey in 1881 in Stockdale, Ohio. He played baseball for the St. Louis Browns and the New York Highlanders. Rickey only played in 120 games, with a career batting average of .239. He managed the St. Louis Browns for three seasons, from 1913 to 1915, and later became the manager of the St. Louis Cardinals, from 1919 to 1925. After 1925, Rickey continued with the Cardinals as the team's general manager.

While with the Cardinals, he developed the farm system, in which young players were trained and groomed for playing in the major leagues. During the 1930s and early 1940s, the Cardinals won several World Series, and many players on those teams had come up through the Cardinals' farm system. Rickey also introduced the idea that players should wear helmets to protect their heads, now a standard practice for batters in a game.

The famous story was recounted somewhat differently by Rickey to Robinson: Thomas had started to cry in the hotel room, and scratching his hands, sobbed, "It's my hands. They're black. If only they were white, I'd be as good as anybody then, wouldn't I, Mr. Rickey? If only they were white."

The experience stuck with Rickey, for whom segregation and racial discrimination were un-Christian acts; he felt called to help African Americans—and anyone who suffered hatred—achieve equality. When he joined the Brooklyn Dodgers as general manager in 1942, he decided to launch a project he had contemplated for some time.

☆ ☆ ☆ ☆ ☆

In 1942, Rickey left the Cardinals and came to the Brooklyn Dodgers as president and general manager. There, he embarked upon the "Noble Experiment" of integrating professional baseball.

While in college, Rickey earned a law degree; perhaps this background was instrumental as he investigated why African Americans were barred from playing professionally. The color barrier was not a written rule but merely a policy that was generally understood. An admirer of Abraham Lincoln, who emancipated African Americans, Rickey wanted to do something to advance civil rights while also allowing him to select the best players for his teams, irrespective of race.

When he signed Jackie Robinson, Rickey was widely criticized, but he stuck by his decision and his vision. When he was general manager of the Pittsburgh Pirates in the 1950s, he drafted Roberto Clemente, who would go on to be the first Hispanic star in the major leagues. In 1967, Rickey was inducted into the Baseball Hall of Fame, two years after his death.

"The Noble Experiment," as he referred to it, was a plan to integrate baseball in a slow, steady way. First, he would find the best African-American baseball player he could, draft him to play for the Dodgers' farm team, the Montreal Royals, and then bring him up into the major leagues. The player selected had to meet two criteria: 1) he had to be an excellent player, so that nobody would question his ability; and 2) he had to be willing to suffer abuse and taunting on and off the playing field. In other words, he had to be capable of handling the tremendous pressure that would result from being the first African-American baseball player in the modern era of major-league baseball. (During the 1880s, two African Americans played briefly in the major leagues.)

The ultimate goal, in Rickey's mind, was that, if this player could prove himself to be patient, upstanding, and dedicated to the sport, he could help open the doors for other African-American players to be accepted and drafted by other teams.

Rickey assigned the Dodgers' scouts to start studying the players on the various Negro League teams. When people became curious as to why Rickey's scouts were looking at African-American players, Rickey lied by saying that he was planning to create a team called the Brooklyn Brown Dodgers, which would play in the Negro National League, and that he was searching for players. The lie diverted attention from what he was doing.

One of Rickey's scouts soon reported that Jackie Robinson seemed like the most promising player for Rickey's "Noble Experiment." In August 1945, at a game in Chicago, as Robinson was warming up, a scout called him over and introduced himself. He said that Rickey wanted to meet him.

Robinson did not raise his hopes. He had heard that Rickey was scouting for a planned Negro League team, but he was curious about why Rickey wanted to meet him in person. "Blacks had to learn to protect themselves by being cynical," he wrote in his autobiography, "but not cynical enough to slam the door on

On October 23, 1945, Jackie Robinson signed a contract to play for the Brooklyn Dodgers organization. He would play his first year with the Dodgers farm team, the Montreal Royals. With him as he signed the contract were *(from left)* Hector Racine, president of the Royals; Branch Rickey, Jr., the Dodgers' farm-system director and son of Branch Rickey; and Romeo Gauvreau, vice president of the Royals.

potential opportunities." Therefore, he agreed to the meeting, which took place in New York on August 28.

The first question Rickey asked him was: "You got a girl?"

Surprised, Robinson nevertheless told him about Rachel and about their plans to get married.

Rickey seemed pleased: "You know, you *have* a girl. When we get through today you may want to call her up because there are times when a man needs a woman by his side." It was then that Rickey told Robinson that he wanted him to play not for the Brooklyn Brown Dodgers but for the Brooklyn Dodgers. He explained the "Noble Experiment" and said that he wanted Robinson to be the first African American to play in the major leagues.

Robinson was thrilled until Rickey added a caveat: "I know you're a good ballplayer. What I don't know is whether you have the guts." Robinson protested, thinking that Rickey was implying he was a coward, but Rickey explained what he meant:

> We can't fight our way through this, Robinson. We've got no army. There's virtually nobody on our side. No owners, no umpires, very few newspapermen. And I'm afraid that many fans will be hostile. We'll be in a tough position. We can win only if we can convince the world that I'm doing this because you're a great ballplayer and a fine gentleman.

Essentially, Rickey wanted Robinson to not respond to racial slurs, hostile remarks, and even violent acts on the field; he feared that, if Robinson reacted angrily to such insults, he would be viewed negatively by already prejudiced reporters and fans. As Rickey stated it, he did not want someone who was afraid to fight back but "a ballplayer with guts enough not to fight back." Robinson said he could do it. To test him, Rickey—in a display that shocked and startled Robinson—stood up and gave him a sampling of the terrible things people might say to him. "He talked about my race, my parents, in language that was almost unbearable," Robinson said. Robinson, however, knew that the Noble Experiment could work, and if it did, it could revolutionize the game of baseball.

On October 23, 1945, Jackie Robinson signed a contract to play for the Brooklyn Dodgers organization. He would receive

Jackie Robinson and Rachel Isum were married on February 10, 1946, at the Independent Church in Los Angeles. Rachel Robinson's support would be crucial to her husband, particularly during his next few pioneering years.

a $3,500 signing bonus, as well as a salary of $600 a month. As agreed upon with Rickey, he would play the first year for the Montreal Royals.

Before the season began, Jackie and Rachel were married on February 10, 1946, in Los Angeles. The Reverend Downs traveled from Texas to perform the ceremony. Rickey was right—Robinson would need the support of a spouse to help him through the next difficult years.

Making History

Jackie Robinson's season with the Montreal Royals had a negative start. Spring training began on March 1 and was held in Florida. After that, Jackie and Rachel would move to Montreal, Canada, to live during the playing season. Their trip from California to Florida, however, was filled with obstacles, reminding Jackie Robinson of how deeply entrenched Jim Crow laws were in the South.

The Robinsons were denied plane seats, even though they had paid for their tickets. Then, they had to stay in a shabby hotel until the airline called to tell them that seats were finally available on a subsequent flight. In Florida, during a bus ride to the training camp, they were ordered to the very rear of the bus, to comply with segregation. They suffered other indignities along the way, which caused them to arrive—flustered, tired, and upset—at spring training a full day late.

It was not a good way for Robinson to begin his career. "I never want another trip like that one," he confided to the sportswriters who were on hand to greet him.

Furthermore, Jackie and Rachel Robinson were not permitted to stay in the same housing facilities as the other players and their families. They stayed instead in the homes of local black families, which allowed them little privacy. Sportswriters hounded Robinson during his first day of training: "Jack, do you think you can get along with these white boys?" he was asked. Robinson fielded the questions gracefully, pointing out that he had played on integrated teams throughout his high school and college career and that he did not expect any problems now. He was asked, "What would you do if one of these pitchers threw at your head?" He replied that he would duck. His sense of humor and candor won over many members of the press.

But that was just talk for the press. Robinson knew full well that many of the Royals players resented him because of his race. He sensed resistance and coldness from many teammates. Then, during one of the first preseason games, he hit his first home run, with two men on base. "This was the day the dam burst between me and my teammates," he wrote later. "Northerners and Southerners alike, they let me know how much they appreciated the way I had come through." His home run clinched the game for the Royals.

Although the fans and his teammates warmed up to him, Robinson still faced problems. One problem was his manager, Clay Hopper, who was racist. Branch Rickey once described a smart play by Robinson as "superhuman," to which Hopper responded incredulously, "Do you really think a [black person is] a human being?" His attitude reflected

Montreal Royals outfielder George Shuba congratulated Jackie Robinson as he crossed home plate after hitting a home run during his first game with the Royals on April 18, 1946. Robinson had four hits in five at-bats, and the Royals defeated the Jersey City Giants that day, 14-1.

the way many people felt—that African Americans were not equal to white people and did not deserve the same treatment or dignity.

During road trips, the entire team often suffered because it included an African-American player. Many times, other teams would cancel their games or find an excuse not to play the Royals; the underlying reason was, of course, that Robinson was black and many teams were based in areas where integrated playing was illegal.

Robinson also faced taunts and slurs from other players. During a game in Syracuse, New York, an opposing player threw a black cat out of the dugout and yelled, "Hey, Jackie, there's your cousin." Remembering Rickey's entreaty not to lose his temper, Robinson instead channeled his anger into his playing. When he next went to bat, he hit a double and then scored a run on a teammate's hit. When he passed the Syracuse dugout, he told the player who had thrown the cat, "I guess my cousin's pretty happy now."

In his debut with the Royals, at Jersey City, New Jersey, Robinson had a spectacular day, getting four hits in five at-bats, including a home run. He stole second base twice and scored four runs. By June, he was an established presence in Montreal. Still, on the road, he suffered abuse from rival players and fans—both subtle and crude. The toll caused by incidents like the black cat in Syracuse "was greater than I realized," Robinson admitted, according to Rampersad's book. "I was overestimating my stamina and underestimating the beating I was taking. I couldn't sleep and often I couldn't eat."

His play, though, was unaffected. He batted .349 in 1946, becoming the first Royal to win the league's batting title. He also scored more runs than anyone else in the league, and his total of 40 stolen bases was good for second place. The Royals won the International League title and then took the "Little World Series," defeating Louisville of the American Association. Robinson scored the winning run in the seventh and deciding game. There was no doubt that Rickey had chosen a player of outstanding merit for his Noble Experiment. After the debut season with the Royals was over, the Robinsons had further reason to celebrate: Their first child, Jackie Robinson, Jr., was born on November 18, 1946.

HISTORY AT EBBETS FIELD

On April 9, 1947, reporters in the Dodgers' press box received a curt announcement, handed out on a sheet of paper: "Brooklyn announces the purchase of the contract of Jack Roosevelt Robinson from Montreal." It was signed by Rickey.

Robinson had been called up from the Royals, and the local and national newspapers across the country exploded with headlines about the history-making event. For the first time in the modern era, an African American would be playing on a team in the major leagues. Two groups of people were not happy about this move.

The first group included the team owners in the Negro Leagues and even some of the players. Their perspective was that the acceptance of African-American players into the professional leagues would spell disaster for the Negro Leagues. The players had built their careers there, and many of them were famous because of it. The owners saw their future profits threatened, and ballpark owners across the country realized that, should the Negro Leagues evaporate, so would a substantial amount of income, since they rented their parks to the teams. The African-American media stepped in at this point to silence any criticism, making it known that the team owners would be ravaged in the press should they vocally oppose the integration of professional baseball. Many players in the Negro Leagues also supported Robinson and Rickey in this history-making endeavor.

The second group of people included major-league players, especially those who played for the Dodgers and would be Robinson's teammates. In one game during spring training in 1947 in Cuba, the Royals played the Dodgers; players on the Dodgers, worried that Rickey would promote Robinson to their team, took out their anger against Robinson on the field. During the game, the Dodgers' catcher, Bruce Edwards, deliberately ran into Robinson, who was covering first base. The impact knocked Robinson to the ground—and rendered him unconscious.

☆ ☆ ☆ ☆ ☆ ☆

A LIFE OF FIRSTS

Throughout his career, Jackie Robinson became the "first" African American to achieve many feats in baseball.

Besides being the first African American to play in a major-league game (in the modern era), on April 15, 1947, he was the first African-American player to steal home plate, a feat accomplished in his first season. He was also the first Rookie of the Year, again in 1947. The first African-American player to lead a league in stolen bases, with 29, he was also one of the first to appear in a World Series game (along with Dan Bankhead). Both of those accomplishments were also in 1947.

In 1949, along with Roy Campanella and Don Newcombe, Robinson was one of the first African-American players to appear in an All-Star Game. Also that year, he was the first African-American player to win the Most Valuable Player award and was the first to lead his league in batting average; he led the National League with a .342 average.

Before he died, Robinson said that he would like to see an African American be a manager in the game that he loved so much. Only then, he believed, would baseball be fully integrated. Though Jackie Robinson did not live to see it, in 1975, Frank Robinson (who was no relation) became the first African-American major-league manager when he took over the management of the Cleveland Indians. A year later, Bill Lucas became the first African-American major-league general manager, for the Atlanta Braves.

Jackie Robinson posed with some of his Brooklyn Dodger teammates on April 15, 1947—the day of his debut in the major leagues. They were *(from left)* John Jorgensen, Pee Wee Reese, and Ed Stanky. Early in the season, Robinson's teammates treated him civilly, at best. Then, as they saw the taunts he had to endure, they began to band together in his defense.

Also while Robinson was still with the Royals, a rumor circulated that the Dodger players were signing a petition to keep Robinson off the team. Behind the petition was a threat that, if the team signed Robinson, the petitioners would refuse to play.

When Rickey got word of the plan, he was furious. He wanted to put down the revolt in as decisive a way as possible. Later he would recall that "a little show of force at the right time is necessary when there's a deliberate violation of law." He asked his team manager, Leo Durocher, who was known for his temper, to settle the issue. Durocher exploded: One night, he dragged the players out of their beds and yelled at them, "I'm the manager of this team, and I say he plays." Then he added something that Robinson would later realize was the single issue that made the big difference in terms of his acceptance: "What's more, I say he can make us a lot of money."

Some team members still refused to play with an African-American player, so they asked to be traded. Others accepted him, but grudgingly. They did not welcome him as a fellow player, and they ignored him in the locker room, in the dugout, and during practice. One player who did reach out to him was shortstop Pee Wee Reese, a native of Kentucky who was eager to play and earn a good salary and who felt that Robinson "had a right to be there, too."

Robinson, assigned No. 42, debuted with the Brooklyn Dodgers on April 15, 1947, playing first base in a game against the Boston Braves. He was nervous about his performance and about the way in which his teammates, the fans, and the opposing team would treat him. Bracing himself for anything—from booing to hostility, as Rickey had warned him could occur—he headed to Ebbets Field and put on his jersey. Rachel Robinson attended the game with their son, even though Jackie, Jr., was very young and they had just made the hasty move from Montreal to New York. She was determined, though, not "to miss the game, after all we had been through," she recalled later.

Jackie Robinson's fears were realized: He did not perform well in the game. Later, he would write, "I did a miserable job. . . . I was in another slump." Though the Dodgers won the game against the Braves (and the next one), Robinson's performance was far below the hyped-up expectations. Devastated, Robinson hoped that he had not disappointed Rickey, who had staked a lot on bringing Robinson up to the majors. Robinson's play did not improve over the next several games: "I went to the plate 20 times without one base hit," he wrote in his memoirs.

Finally, in a series against the New York Giants, Robinson returned to his typical on-field form. In that series, he had five hits, including a home run. He played his position at first base without a single error, performing gracefully. Sports reporters were impressed with his poise, as well as the polite, easy way in which he answered their questions after the games. The fans were also impressed with Robinson; in one of the games against the Giants, a record was set for the largest crowd to attend a game at the Polo Grounds on a Saturday. "They came to see Jackie Robinson," one radio station stated simply. He became the biggest attraction in baseball since Babe Ruth.

RACISM ON THE FIELD

While Robinson became more comfortable playing on the Dodgers and while the fans and press warmed up to him, he still faced hostility from other players. His relationship with his Dodgers teammates was civil but cool—few players were friendly to him. One reporter described Robinson as "the loneliest man I have ever seen in sports." The players on opposing teams often acted with aggression and ignorance toward the Dodgers' new first baseman.

One game against the Philadelphia Phillies has become renowned as one of the worst in terms of racial aggression. The Phillies were in Brooklyn for a three-game series against the Dodgers, and their manager, Ben Chapman, an Alabama native, wanted to make sure that Robinson knew he was not welcome in professional baseball. During the first game, on April 22, as

Robinson headed out to the field, he heard comments emanating from the Phillies dugout that shocked him:

> Hey, why don't you go back to the cotton field where you belong?
> They're waiting for you in the jungles, black boy!
> Hey, snowflake, which one of those white boys' wives are you dating tonight?
> Go back to the bushes!

In his memoirs, Robinson said that day was one of the most torturous of his life, a day that "brought me nearer to cracking up than I ever had been. For one wild and rage-crazed minute I thought, 'To hell with Mr. Rickey's "Noble Experiment." It's clear it won't succeed.' " He felt the urge to walk over to the Phillies' dugout and fight with the players who taunted him. At the last minute, however, he remembered that this situation was exactly what Rickey had warned him about more than a year before, when he had mimicked what he would hear from other players on the field. This prediction had come true in the worst way, but back then, Robinson had promised he could deal with it. And he did—he ignored the Phillies players and manager and instead he channeled his anger and frustration into his playing. In that series, he hit well and even scored the winning run in the first game (after hitting to first, and then stealing second and third).

The Phillies kept up their nasty comments and taunts until even the other Dodger players could not stand it. One player, Ed Stanky, became furious: "Listen, you yellow-bellied cowards, why don't you yell at somebody who can answer back?" The media also picked up on the incident and wrote scathingly of Chapman, recalling earlier anti-Semitic remarks he had made as well. The situation depicted Chapman and the Phillies in a harsh light, while Robinson was seen as a patient, hard-working victim of abuse. One reporter called him "the only gentleman among those involved in the incident."

The Dodgers swept the Phillies in the series. An even sweeter success was that Robinson now felt that his teammates stood behind him—they had become angry at seeing one of their own taunted by a rival team. Rickey later described the irony by saying that "Chapman did more than anybody to unite the Dodgers." Later, to settle the issue, Robinson agreed to take a goodwill photo with Chapman for the press; he agreed to do so only reluctantly, however. "I have to admit, though," he later wrote, "that having my picture taken with this man was one of the most difficult things I had to make myself do."

That photo opportunity hardly signaled the end of racism on the field for Robinson, however. The St. Louis Cardinals were coming to Brooklyn for a series, and a plot brewed to prevent Robinson from playing. The Cardinals players planned a strike, threatening not to play in the game if Robinson took the field. The real danger, as Robinson later said, was that, if the plan was successful, it "could have had a chain reaction throughout the baseball world—with other players agreeing to unite in a strong bid to keep baseball white."

The plot was exposed in the press, however, and the president of the National League, Ford Frick, warned the Cardinals players that he would not tolerate a strike:

> If you do this, you will be suspended from the league. You will find that the friends you think you have in the press box will not support you, that you will be outcasts. I do not care if half the league strikes. Those who do it will encounter quick retribution. They will be suspended and I don't care if it wrecks the National League for five years. This is the United States of America, and one citizen has as much right to play as another. . . . The National League will go down the line with Robinson whatever the consequence. You will find

Umpire George Magerkurth motioned Jackie Robinson to first base after he was hit on the left arm by a pitch in a game in June 1947 against the Pittsburgh Pirates. Before the end of May in his first season, Robinson had been hit by pitches six times. During the entire previous season, no National League player was hit more than six times.

if you go through with your intention that you have been guilty of complete madness.

Frick's strong, assertive language was probably motivated by the notion that a strike by many of the teams in the league would set a precedent; whenever anything dissatisfied the players, they would know that strikes had an effect, which would hurt the financial investments of team owners. Whatever the reason, Frick's support effectively foiled the Cardinals' plot and any ideas that other teams might have had about resisting the integration of baseball.

Still, Frick's action, of course, did not stop players from hurling negative comments and racist remarks at Robinson. Sometimes, they did worse: During a game against the St. Louis Cardinals, Enos Slaughter hit a ground ball and headed for first. A Dodger infielder caught the ball and threw it to Robinson at first base to make the out, but as Robinson reached to catch it, Slaughter "deliberately went for my leg instead of the base and spiked me rather severely." It was one of many, many instances in which Robinson suffered intentional spikes, hits, and jabs on the field. Biographer Arnold Rampersad notes, "In the thirty-seven games played before the end of May, Jack was hit by pitches six times; in the entire 1946 season, no National League player had been hit by pitches more than six times." Despite the blatant abuse, Robinson could do nothing about it because, as Rickey said, it would tarnish his reputation and make him seem like a complainer. The goal, Rickey reminded him, was to show the world that he was a first-class player who could handle any problem he encountered with dignity and grace.

Indeed, Robinson's teammates became advocates for their first baseman. They saw what he had to handle, and they often defended him, changing the atmosphere among the ball club in Robinson's favor. For example, when Slaughter spiked Robinson's leg, many Dodger players "came charging out of [the dugout] on the field to protest. . . . [T]he spirit shown after the Slaughter incident strengthened our resolve and made us go on to win the pennant," Robinson wrote in his memoir. Whatever they had felt about Robinson when he first joined the team, the Dodger players grew to view him as one of their own, and they banded together in his defense.

A Public Figure

During this distressing time, Rachel Robinson realized that her husband's torture on the field by other players weighed heavily on his mind. She recalled that her husband's concerns "were eating at his mind, for he would jerk and twitch and even talk in his troubled sleep, which was not like him." He tried to maintain a pleasant and confident attitude in front of his wife and their small son, but Jackie Robinson was a troubled person, torn by his desire to defend his dignity and his conflicting desire to keep his promise to Branch Rickey. "Not being able to fight back is a form of severe punishment," he would write in his memoir.

Underlying all of this tension was his knowledge that the results of the "Noble Experiment" would affect the future of

Jackie and Rachel Robinson admire the new car he received during Jackie Robinson Day at Ebbets Field in Brooklyn at the end of his first season. The Brooklyn Dodgers won the National League pennant in 1947 but fell to the New York Yankees in the World Series.

African Americans in baseball. Indeed, other teams had started to sign African Americans to their clubs by this point, but the spotlight in the media continued to focus on Robinson and his every success and failure.

Robinson learned to direct his anger into his performance, which had been less than stellar in his first months with the Dodgers. He started to turn his game around in June, when he began a 21-game hitting streak. On June 24, 1947, the Dodgers faced Pittsburgh and pitcher Fritz Ostermueller, who earlier in the season had thrown a ball at Robinson's head. This game, after he got on base, Robinson stole home for the first time in the major leagues, driving the crowd into a frenzy. After all, his base stealing was his trademark in the minor leagues, and now he was unleashing his baserunning abilities to the advantage of the Dodgers.

By September, the Dodgers were in the race for the National League pennant, which thrilled the Brooklyn fans. They knew that they owed a significant part of this achievement to Robinson. The nation also recognized Robinson's achievements: On September 22, *Time* magazine featured a picture of Robinson on its cover.

On September 23, the Dodgers and *The People's Voice* newspaper declared it "Jackie Robinson Day" at Ebbets Field. Robinson's mother, Mallie Robinson, and his mentor, the Reverend Karl Downs, flew into town to be at the event, during which Robinson was presented with several gifts, including a new television and a new Cadillac.

Three days later, *Sporting News* presented Robinson with its "Rookie of the Year Award," adding, "The sociological experiment that Robinson represented, the trail-blazing that he did, did not enter into the decision. He was rated and examined solely as a freshman player in the big leagues—on the basis of his hitting, his running, his defensive play, his team value."

Besides the *Sporting News* award, Robinson was also named Major League Baseball's Rookie of the Year—in the first season the award was presented. *Sporting News* had originally decried and opposed the integration of professional baseball. Robinson was beginning to win over many enemies. In November, a national survey ranked him as one of the most popular and well-liked Americans, more admired than President Harry Truman, General Douglas MacArthur, and entertainer Bob Hope.

LOSSES

The Dodgers won the National League pennant in 1947, and their opponents in the World Series were their archrivals and neighbors, the New York Yankees. Robinson was very excited, especially because it was his first year playing in the major leagues and he had contributed to his team's success in getting this far. Despite a good show by all of the Dodgers, the all-star lineup of the Yankees, which included Joe DiMaggio, defeated Brooklyn in seven games.

Disappointed, Robinson was nevertheless uplifted at the end of a season that had been grueling in more ways than one.

He signed a contract for the 1948 season with the Dodgers, hoping to earn a large raise. Robinson was paid $5,000, the minimum amount allowed, in 1947. He was not happy with his new salary, $12,500, but he did not complain to Rickey; the salary was not the highest in the league, but it was comparable to what his Dodger teammates were earning.

Early in 1948, Jackie and Rachel were crushed to learn that the Reverend Karl Downs had passed away. They were even more upset to learn of the circumstances surrounding his death. Ailing from stomach problems, he was admitted on February 26 to Brackenridge Hospital in Austin, Texas, for emergency surgery. The hospital was segregated, and even though Downs suffered from complications after surgery, he was not allowed to remain in a recovery room for observation, a decision made by his white doctor. Instead, he was sent back to the segregated ward, which did not have the same quality of care as the white section of the hospital. He died in that ward, a victim of Jim Crow segregation, which had even tarnished medical ethics. He was 35 years old.

"It was hard to believe that God had taken the life of a man with such a promising future," Robinson said. Downs's death rocked him emotionally, stirring up memories of the death of his brother Frank. It also sparked in him a staunch desire to act out against the vicious social system of Jim Crow, which had taken the life of his friend and mentor.

EARNING A LIVING

Robinson's first season with the Dodgers had made history and generated extra income for the organization, with fans flooding the stands at almost every game to see him play. Very little of that money, however, was given to Robinson, who knew he should start earning extra money any way possible to provide for his family. Since "Jackie Robinson" was now a name known by almost every American—and admired by most of them—he decided to cash in on his popularity.

He accepted a number of endorsement deals, appearing in commercials and advertisements for everything from Homogenized Bond bread to Old Gold cigarettes. He also entertained offers for movie and book deals. A hastily completed autobiography, ghostwritten by journalist Wendell Smith and entitled *Jackie Robinson: My Own Story*, was published in May 1948, but it contained many errors that upset Robinson, including his mother being called "Mollie" instead of "Mallie" and Robinson's own name appearing as "John Roosevelt Robinson." The many errors embarrassed Jackie, who was listed as the author.

He also used his popularity for the benefit of charitable causes. As an observant Christian, Robinson believed that he was obligated to help society and to uplift people in need in any way he could. He agreed to appear as a guest speaker at fundraising dinners and events for several organizations, and his name attracted many people to the benefits. He spent a lot of time visiting sick children, many of them terminally ill, at

Jackie Robinson slid safely into third base after hitting a triple to center field in a June 1948 game against the Chicago Cubs at Ebbets Field. Robinson hit .296 in his second season with the Dodgers, but overall, he was disappointed with his performance in 1948.

hospitals across the country; the children enjoyed a visit from one of baseball's most famous players. One young boy said, "Gee, Jackie Robinson, and he came here just to see me." In his charitable efforts, Robinson made no distinction between black and white causes; he visited black and white children alike, and he helped raise money for organizations that served both communities.

OUT OF SHAPE

One result of Robinson's busy schedule in the off-season, before the 1948 campaign began, was that he arrived at training camp terribly out of shape at 215 pounds (97.5 kilograms). He was "too fat to be effective," sportswriters mused, and his appearance shocked his manager.

Robinson swore that he would never again allow himself to succumb to the temptations of lavish dinners and excessive eating. He worked hard during the training season to get back into shape, and he quickly lost most of the weight he had accumulated, getting down to 200 pounds (91 kilograms). It was a sobering lesson learned.

During the season, racist incidents continued; he led the league in being hit by pitched balls, "a dubious distinction," as he said in his memoir. However, he also became more vocal about protesting injustices; though he did not engage in fights with players who abused or taunted him, he did once get ejected from a game by an umpire for railing against what he considered to be a bad call. For Robinson, it was a triumph: He finally felt comfortable expressing himself on the field. "He didn't pick on me because I was black," Robinson later recalled happily. "He was treating me exactly as he would any ballplayer who got on his nerves. That made me feel great."

Although he worked hard, the 1948 season was hardly his best. He was now playing second base, his preferred position. (Brooklyn had traded the previous second baseman.) Nagging injuries affected him in the field, but he ended up batting .296 for the season, just below his rookie-year average of .297. Robinson, though, knew he could have done much better, and starting the season in such poor shape had not helped. "Deep in my heart I was miserable," he wrote, "because I knew that I should have done better—much better."

When the 1948 season ended, he vowed to remain in shape by playing on a barnstorming tour, along with Roy

Campanella, another African-American player whom the Dodgers had signed. Barnstorming was a great tradition among black baseball teams: Most of the Negro League teams would travel around the country, picking up games with other teams wherever and whenever they could. It was a good way to earn money. The games exhibited tremendous playing and were affordable enough that many fans attended.

In 1948, Jackie and Rachel Robinson also moved into a house in Brooklyn, in the Flatbush section. The house was owned by an African-American woman, and the white residents of the neighborhood had initially tried to block her purchase of the house. They were also unhappy when the Robinsons moved in. Some neighbors were welcoming, however, and reached out to the young family. Some of these neighbors would become lifelong friends of the Robinsons.

Soon, Rachel Robinson began to hunt for a new house again, and she discovered a home in the St. Albans section of Queens in New York City. The Robinsons purchased their first home there and settled in to get ready for the 1949 season.

TESTIMONY IN WASHINGTON

The 1949 season began well for Robinson. Although he was hoping for a salary of $20,000 a year, Branch Rickey raised his salary to $17,500. It was a compromise, and Robinson was satisfied.

During the training season, the Dodgers played some exhibition games in the South, where they ran into problems with Jim Crow laws again. The Ku Klux Klan had become more powerful than ever in the Deep South, especially in Robinson's native state of Georgia. During a scheduled series of games in Atlanta in early April, the Ku Klux Klan threatened to stop the playing of integrated baseball. In response, Robinson insisted, "I will play baseball where my employer, the Brooklyn Dodgers, wants me to play." The games were

played as scheduled, and although he was booed by ι.
Robinson played very well; by the end, he heard some c̄9
for him coming from the stands.

During the season, he started off slowly but picked up by
early summer. He was named to play in the All-Star Game,
receiving the second-highest number of fan votes. Although
the National League team lost to the American League,
Robinson was excited to be playing in the game and to have
been recognized.

Shortly before the All-Star Game, however, Robinson was
recognized in quite a different way, perhaps in a way he did not
prefer. On July 8, 1949, he was called to testify before the House
Un-American Activities Committee (HUAC). Led by U.S.
Representative John S. Wood of Georgia, the mission of HUAC
was to investigate American citizens who had been accused of
behaving in ways that were detrimental to the United States.
The existence of the committee was a testament to the high
level of anti-communist sentiment in the country at the time.

Communism, as embodied by the United States' chief
political enemy at the time, the Soviet Union, went against the
American system of capitalism, and many in the United States
believed that those who held communist views were a threat.
Some African Americans, however, supported communist
views, for a variety of reasons. Some believed that it was capitalism, the system in which making money was the chief goal,
that had allowed slavery to exist for so long; as long as people
were profiting from the sale of other human beings, there was
no real reason to abolish the system. Some African Americans
liked communism's emphasis on equality for the masses: In
theory, socialism (of which communism is an outgrowth) pur-
ports that all humans are equal; it eliminates all major socio-
economic differences between people, such as class, race, and
even gender. Many African Americans had visited European
countries, like France, where socialism was influential, and

they had been amazed at the level of equal treatment they had received. Many of these prominent African Americans, like the writers Richard Wright and James Baldwin, even left the United States and made France their permanent home.

Others, like Paul Robeson, the noted African-American singer and actor, experienced the same treatment when they

☆ ☆ ☆ ☆ ☆

THE HOUSE UN-AMERICAN ACTIVITIES COMMITTEE

When Jackie Robinson was called to testify before the House Un-American Activities Committee (HUAC), it may have surprised him and his family, but many other people, especially celebrities, had received a similar summons.

The committee, formed in the United States House of Representatives, was established in 1938, a few years before the country entered World War II. Its purpose was to investigate groups or people who were thought to be disloyal to the United States and who might possibly be working to harm U.S. interests. Initially, the committee was charged to investigate activities of the Ku Klux Klan, but it did very little to this effect. It was also supposed to have looked into whether the Nazis were spreading their pro-German propaganda in the United States, but it also failed to achieve much in this regard. Eventually, by the time it became a permanent committee in 1946, the HUAC was working almost exclusively to investigate communist groups or people in the United States who had communist sympathies.

Many of the people alleged to be communist sympathizers were Hollywood elites, such as movie directors, actors, and producers. In 1947, the HUAC subpoenaed 10 people who worked in the movie industry to appear and testify before the committee; these writers and directors, known as the "Hollywood Ten," visited the Soviet Union, where communism was the established economic system. In April 1949, Robeson made a statement before an audience gathered at the World Congress of the Partisans of Peace, held in Paris. He said, "It is unthinkable that American Negroes would go to war on behalf of those who have oppressed us for generations against a country in which

refused, knowing that they would be accused and interrogated about their alleged connection to and support of the American Communist Party. Soon after, the Motion Picture Association of America fired them and they were put on a "blacklist," meaning that their names were circulated to others in the industry. They had a difficult time finding work in Hollywood after the blacklisting, and many of them even had to leave the United States to find jobs. Some of them, however, continued to work, but under false names or pseudonyms.

Many people were called before the HUAC and were asked to reveal the names of others, friends and colleagues, who might have been communist sympathizers. This tactic, for which a person could be held in contempt of Congress for refusing to do, was questioned by others and considered un-American. In supposedly defending the American system of government and way of life, the HUAC was using strategies that violated the rights of its own citizens.

After the 1950s, the work and methods of the HUAC came under closer scrutiny from the American public, and the committee's importance began to fade. It is remembered today as one of the most powerful government bodies formed during the height of the "red scare."

one generation had raised our people to the full dignity of mankind." Many Americans interpreted the comment to mean that, should the United States and the Soviet Union ever go to war, African Americans would refuse to fight on the side of the U.S. military as a protest of the Jim Crow system and the history of racism in the United States.

The comment alarmed many to the point that they wanted confirmation from other prominent African Americans that this idea—however improbable—was not actually the case. This was the reason why Jackie Robinson was called by Congressman Wood to testify. Robinson again found himself in the position of being a representative of the African-American community.

With this representation came major responsibility: How could he speak for a community that held a wide range of views? The simple answer, he realized, was that he could not. He could only speak for himself and put forth his own personal views. Furthermore, he did not want to speak out against a man like Paul Robeson, who had used his celebrity and fame to fight against racism and segregation; in fact, Robeson had been an advocate of the integration of professional baseball. When he had heard that the Dodgers had signed Robinson, Robeson had declared it "the greatest step ever taken by organized baseball on behalf of the American Negro." "Now," Robinson said later of the experience, "a white man from Georgia was asking *me*, a 'refugee' from Georgia, to denounce Robeson." The situation was truly ironic, and Robinson did not want to mar his career by making a wrong move.

He wrote and reviewed his testimony many times, seeking the advice of his friends and of Rachel, who had recently found out she was pregnant. He knew that his statement would be circulated widely and be the focus of the media, so he was very careful about what he said. When he appeared before the House Un-American Activities Committee in Washington, D.C., on July 18, he delivered his testimony in

Jackie Robinson is shown testifying on July 18, 1949, before the House Un-American Activities Committee in Washington, D.C. He was asked to appear before the committee to respond to comments made by actor Paul Robeson that alarmed many in Washington. Robinson's testimony was widely praised.

plain language, as he was a direct person who disliked fancy speeches. He made several important points, including stating that communists were not rallying African Americans against their country:

> Every single Negro who is worth his salt is going to resent any kind of slurs and discrimination because of his race, and he's going to use every bit of intelligence, such as he has, to stop it. This has got absolutely nothing to do with what communists may or may not be trying to do. . . . [B]ecause it is a communist who denounces injustice in the courts, police brutality and lynching, when it happens, doesn't change the truth of his charges.

Rather than railing and denouncing Robeson, as the committee seemed to want him to do, Robinson dismissed Robeson's remarks with a brief comment: "I haven't any comment to make, except that the statement, if Mr. Robeson actually made it, sounds very silly to me." As a former member of the military, Robinson believed that African Americans, if called upon by their country to serve and defend it, would do so unhesitatingly, just as they had in previous wars. Before his appearance, Robinson had told himself, "I didn't want to fall prey to the white man's game and allow myself to be pitted against another black man." Indeed, he eluded that trap completely. He concluded by saying:

> I am a religious man. Therefore I cherish America where I am free to worship as I please, a privilege which some countries do not give. And I suspect that nine hundred and ninety-nine out of almost any thousand colored Americans you meet will tell you the same thing. But that doesn't mean that we're going to stop fighting race discrimination in this country until we've got it licked. It means that we're going to fight it all the harder because our stake in the future is so big. We can win our fight without the communists, and we don't want their help.

When he finished making his statement, Jackie and Rachel Robinson quickly left the hearing room and flew back to New

York. The Dodgers played the Cubs that evening, a game that they won 3-0; Robinson thrilled the fans by stealing home.

His statement also thrilled Americans: Many admired the way in which he used his testimony before the committee to criticize the established practice of Jim Crow laws in the United States. "Quite a man, this Jackie Robinson," ran the editorial of the New York *Daily News.* "Quite a ballplayer. And quite a credit, not only to his own race, but to all the American people."

His exploits on the field continued to soar in 1949. He won the National League batting title, with an average of .342—beating out Stan Musial (.339) and Enos Slaughter (.336) of the St. Louis Cardinals. Robinson also led the league in stolen bases with 37. The Dodgers again won the National League pennant, and again, they lost to the New York Yankees in the World Series.

At the end of the 1949 season, Robinson was ecstatic to be named the Most Valuable Player in the National League—it was a tremendous honor, and he was proud of it.

By the end of his third full season with the Dodgers, Jackie Robinson was officially an American hero.

7

Advancing the Race

On January 13, 1950, Rachel Robinson gave birth to the Robinsons' second child, a girl. Elated, Jackie and Rachel named their new addition Sharon. The morning after her birth, Sharon's excited father stood in front of the YMCA building in Harlem and handed out cigars to passersby.

In fact, Jackie Robinson served on the board of directors of the Harlem YMCA, a famous place in the neighborhood that had given shelter to many and initiated programs to advance the community. Robinson, at the pinnacle of his baseball career, had decided to turn his attention to using his fame to help the cause of equality for African Americans as well as to help the community realize the American dream—just as he had.

The era after World War II was a difficult one, however, for African Americans. Poverty still plagued most urban

African-American communities, and unemployment rates were high (though not as high as they would get in the near future). Furthermore, the history of segregation had ensured that schools in African-American neighborhoods received less funding and less attention, which in turn provided students with a less rigorous education. The cycle of poverty was thus perpetuated.

Robinson had always been active in charitable causes that benefited young children, white or black. He wanted, however, to start advocating for ways in which the wider problem of racial discrimination in the United States could be abolished.

One reason Robinson felt so strongly about being involved was that, despite how well he was treated because of his celebrity, he knew that he was the exception rather than the rule. Rachel Robinson shared an understanding with her husband about whether other African Americans were treated as well as Jackie by certain establishments: "One way we knew the answer to that was by looking at how I was treated when I was not with Jack—not with Jackie Robinson. Sometimes I was treated well, but very often, until or unless it came out that I was Jackie Robinson's wife, whites would be as rude to me as they were rude to other blacks. These things upset Jackie pretty badly."

Thus, when community groups and other organizations contacted Jackie Robinson to serve as a guest speaker at a fundraising dinner or to make a special appearance at a children's hospital or community center, the baseball superstar readily accepted the invitation. He would devote much more time to these activities in the future.

THE JACKIE ROBINSON STORY

In Hollywood, the buzz about Jackie Robinson's success in baseball and in making himself a part of American history had not gone unnoticed and, in typical Hollywood style, movie executives were planning to capture it on film.

Before the 1950 season, Jackie Robinson spent some time in Hollywood, starring as himself in the film *The Jackie Robinson Story*. Rehearsing on the set one day were *(from left)* Dewey Robinson, who played a Dodger fan who heckled Jackie; Louise Beavers, who portrayed Jackie's mother; and Jackie Robinson.

As movie contract negotiations ensued, Branch Rickey hired his assistant, Arthur Mann, to oversee the accuracy of any portrayals of Rickey himself. Mann decided to write his own biography of Robinson, even though such a book already existed. The new book would be the basis for the movie, as well as a way to make sure that the publishers of the first book did not try to claim that the movie infringed on their copyright.

The movie budget was only $300,000, which made it a "low-budget" film, but one upside would be that Robinson would play himself. This was an unusual prospect for Robinson, who was not afraid to conquer new challenges. He felt, however, that he needed the support of Rachel, who flew to Los Angeles with Sharon (Jackie, Jr., had already come to Los Angeles with his father) to be by his side on the set.

Filming began in February 1950, and Robinson was stunned that the actors—who included the alluring Ruby Dee, playing the role of Rachel—were expected to work long hours, day and night, to finish shooting within the scheduled amount of time. He never anticipated the rigors of moviemaking; while filming action scenes of baseball games, for example, he had to run the bases several times in a row to get the best shot. Later, he claimed that shooting the film was more demanding than spring training.

The Jackie Robinson Story debuted on May 16, 1950, in New York to packed movie theaters. Many critics liked the film, although some slammed its low-budget quality, which was to be expected, and others disliked the obviousness of the patriotic American theme. Many agreed, however, that Robinson had done an excellent job in his first (and last) acting role, even though he was playing himself. He seemed to possess a natural grace and ease on camera that pleased his audiences.

Robinson also made a good amount of money from the movie, which did well in the theaters. During the 1950 baseball season, his income increased even more when his new salary was announced: At $35,000, he was now the highest-paid Dodger ever.

Although he batted and fielded well, the 1950 season was disappointing to Robinson when compared with his previous MVP season. He was disappointed for other reasons, too.

Because he had been more vocal in recent months about being mistreated, he felt that people had turned against him. When he objected to a bad call by an umpire, he felt the scorn of others for speaking out, although he knew many white players who did the same and received no objections. Again and again, he would be labeled a troublemaker, but he would insist that he was simply asserting his right to speak freely—just because he was an African American playing in the professional leagues did not mean that he should always behave humbly and pretend to be eternally grateful for the opportunity.

Branch Rickey had always supported Robinson's right to defend himself on the field. In mid-season, however, after the death of one of the four Dodger owners, a power struggle broke out between Rickey and Walter O'Malley, who each owned a quarter share of the Dodgers. By season's end, control of the Brooklyn Dodgers came into the hands of O'Malley, and Rickey left the organization. Robinson was shocked and felt abandoned, but he respected Rickey's right to move on. "It has been the finest experience I have had being associated with you and I want to thank you very much for all you have meant not only to me and my family but to the entire country and particularly the members of our race," Robinson wrote to Rickey.

O'Malley's takeover of the ball club had caused a major problem with Rickey; it ended badly, and O'Malley instructed those around him never to utter Rickey's name. Robinson felt that O'Malley disliked him tremendously because of his special relationship with and respect for Rickey. "O'Malley's attitude towards me was viciously antagonistic," he wrote in his memoir. "I learned that he had a habit of calling me Mr. Rickey's prima donna and giving Mr. Rickey a hard time about what kind of season I would have." In fact, O'Malley's takeover of the Dodgers signaled the beginning of the end of Robinson's days in baseball.

MAKING A MOVE

On May 14, 1952, the Robinsons' third child, David, was born. His birth not only made the family even happier than before, it helped them understand that they needed a larger home. They began to hunt for houses, and because the schools in their area were not the best, they decided to look north, in Connecticut. They soon entered a battle against housing discrimination.

Because Robinson was busy with baseball, Rachel Robinson headed the house-hunting endeavor; she received many signals from various communities that black families were not welcome. At one point, she even realized that her real estate agent was trying to talk her out of considering a particular neighborhood because she herself lived there. Rachel Robinson complained of this treatment during a newspaper interview for the *Herald* newspaper in Bridgeport, Connecticut, and various residents of North Stamford, appalled at how she had been treated, acted to help her. They formed a committee to help the Robinsons find a property in their community, and eventually, they succeeded. The Robinsons bought a property in 1954, although the home was not finished until 1955.

While the house hunting was going on, Jackie Robinson continued to experience difficulty with the Dodgers' new ownership. He also continued to battle prejudice. During a youth forum, a young girl asked him about the New York Yankees, who had yet to sign an African-American ballplayer. Robinson replied directly that he felt the Yankee management was prejudiced because it still had very few black players in its farm system, even though many teams in both leagues had signed African-American players since he had entered the major leagues. His comment infuriated the Yankees as well as many fans and sportswriters. He received hate mail and angry phone calls, and at one point, he was called into the office of Ford Frick, who was now the baseball commissioner. Angry,

Jackie Robinson is seen in this portrait from May 1952. The Robinsons' third child, David, was born that month, and with the larger family, Jackie and Rachel Robinson began to think about moving to a bigger home. Within a few years, they were living in Connecticut.

Robinson demanded to know why his comment, which had been truthful, should get him into trouble. Frick surprised him by giving him support. "Jackie," Frick said, "I just want you to know how I feel personally. Whenever you believe enough in something to sound off about it, whenever you feel strongly that you've got to come out swinging, I sincerely hope you'll swing the real heavy bat and not the fungo." That kind of executive-level support surprised Robinson, and it reminded him that times were changing, however slowly.

He would endure more problems. At one point, during the 1952 season, Walter O'Malley called Robinson into his office to berate him for refusing to play in a game because he was injured. O'Malley made an odd request that Rachel also be present, probably because he wanted to embarrass Jackie in front of his own wife. The plan backfired. When he called Jackie a "crybaby" and a "prima donna," both men were shocked when Rachel Robinson was the one who responded.

"That's when Rachel's rage broke," Jackie Robinson recalled.

"Nobody worries about this club more than Jackie Robinson, and that includes the owners," she exploded. "I live with him, so I know. Nobody gets up earlier than Jackie Robinson to see what kind of day it's going to be, if it's going to be good weather for the game, if the team is likely to have a good crowd. . . . Jack's heart and soul is with the baseball club, and it pains me deeply to have you say what you just said."

O'Malley quickly backed off his initial statement, but trouble between him and Jackie Robinson would continue to brew.

THE 1955 WORLD SERIES

Problems also persisted with the team's new managers, who Robinson felt did not support him in his efforts. Still, despite his conflicts with the managers and owners, Robinson had quite productive years during the 1950s. From 1950 to 1954, his batting average never fell below .300—he batted .338 in

In the first game of the 1955 World Series, Jackie Robinson slid under catcher Yogi Berra's mitt to steal home. The Dodgers finally defeated the New York Yankees, their crosstown rivals, in a World Series, but it took all seven games. Robinson was elated to win the Series, but he knew that his time with the Dodgers was nearing its end.

1951 and .329 in 1953. He also made the All-Star Game all those years.

The 1955 season was bittersweet: Robinson hardly played his best, although the team was in the thick of the pennant race. The Dodgers ended up winning the National League title and advanced to the World Series. Unsurprisingly, they faced the Yankees in what was becoming a common occurrence, snarling New York traffic as the two teams squared off on the field.

Since Robinson had joined the team, the Dodgers had been in four World Series (1947, 1949, 1952, and 1953) and had lost them all to the Yankees. The Brooklyn fans did not get their hopes up in 1955, since those hopes had been dashed so often in the past. They were not surprised when the Yankees won the first two games of the World Series.

This year was different, however: The Dodgers rallied and won the third, fourth, and fifth games. Then the Yankees themselves rallied and won the sixth game. The tension was high, and hopes skyrocketed in Brooklyn as the all-important Game 7 approached on October 4. The game was tense, with the Dodgers leading 2-0. Then in the sixth inning, two Yankees made it to base. With a runner at first and one on second, the Yankee power hitter Yogi Berra came up to bat: He hit a long drive to left field, and the Dodgers fans collectively groaned. The hit would probably drive in two runs and leave Berra at third.

In a move that has been labeled the most sensational save in World Series history, the Dodgers' left fielder, Sandy Amorós, ran the ball down and caught it with his left hand, then turned and threw it accurately to shortstop Pee Wee Reese. Reese relayed the ball to first base to put out the base runner for a perfect double play. The Yankees never recovered.

The Dodgers—almost impossibly—shut out the Yankees, 2-0, winning the World Series for the first time in the history of the franchise.

Robinson, perhaps knowing he might not have another chance to play in a World Series, gave it everything he had. In the first game, with his team down, he stole home base, thrilling the fans and his teammates. He did not play in the final game, however. Also, he did not bat well in the series, with only

☆ ☆ ☆ ☆ ☆ ☆

THE DODGERS MOVE TO LOS ANGELES

While Jackie Robinson was contemplating his next move after baseball, the owners of the Brooklyn Dodgers were contemplating a move of their own—from their longtime home in Brooklyn.

The Dodgers were established in 1883 in Brooklyn, a borough in New York City where the citizens took baseball seriously. In 1905, after an administrator tried to move the team to Baltimore, Charles Ebbets, an employee of the club, bought the team (putting himself deep into debt). He furthered his debt by financing the construction of a new ballpark, Ebbets Field, which would become the home of the Dodgers in 1913.

When Walter O'Malley became the majority owner of the team in 1950, he had major ambitions. He wanted to build a better ballpark, one more modern than the aging Ebbets Field. He had problems, however, finding a prime choice of property for the new stadium in Brooklyn.

Officials from Los Angeles had attended the 1955 World Series and decided to make an offer—a chance to buy land for a ballpark—that would enable the Dodgers to move to Los Angeles. O'Malley accepted the offer. The Dodgers played their first game in Los Angeles on April 18, 1958, at the Los Angeles Memorial Coliseum. The move was controversial, with some painting O'Malley as a traitor to Brooklyn. Those in O'Malley's camp blamed New York officials who had made it difficult for the owner to purchase property for a better ballpark. O'Malley, therefore, portrayed himself and the team as having been exiled from Brooklyn. In 1962, the Dodgers began to play in O'Malley's new park, Dodger Stadium.

4 hits in 22 at-bats, for a .182 average. Though he was ecstatic that the Dodgers had won, he knew his own days on the team were numbered.

The 1956 season also did not go very well for him, although his statistics were a bit better than the previous season. Robinson batted .275 in 117 games. Once again, the Dodgers squared off against the Yankees in the World Series, but this time, Brooklyn lost.

"Jack was shaky about his own place with the club," writes biographer Arnold Rampersad. He had been unhappy for some time. In fact, in his own memoir, Robinson wrote simply, "By the end of the 1954 season I was getting fed up and I began to make preparations to leave baseball." By 1956, his thoughts had become even more serious about exiting from the game and starting a new, different career.

8

The Last
Game

At this moment, a business opportunity presented itself, seemingly from heaven: In December 1956, Jackie Robinson met William Black, the owner and founder of the Chock Full o'Nuts coffee company. Black established the company in 1922, when he was a poor young man selling nuts at a stand in an office building in New York City. Within a few years, he had earned some notice and had opened a few small nut shops. He then expanded to selling coffee, sandwiches, and other light fare. Employing blacks and whites, Chock Full o'Nuts had a well-established name and reputation in New York City.

Black wanted Robinson because he thought Robinson could help him with a labor problem: Black was looking for a new director of personnel who could appeal to all of his employees. He did not want his employees to form a union, especially because Black was known for offering fair working conditions with solid benefits. Robinson was intrigued by the prospect of working in a corporation and of being in charge of the welfare of a company's entire employee base. He felt that he could handle the responsibility in a fair and humane manner, plus he could learn many business skills by doing so.

On December 12, 1956, Robinson arrived in Manhattan to sign a contract with William Black. He had not yet told the Dodgers that he would not be returning the next season (he had promised exclusive rights to his retirement story to *Look* magazine, which had not yet released the article). After he signed the contract, which promised him an annual salary of $30,000, he returned a phone call to Buzzie Bavasi, the Dodgers' general manager.

The timing could not have been more fortuitous for Robinson. Bavasi was calling to tell him that the Dodgers had traded him to the New York Giants. Although players are traded all the time, Robinson was insulted that he, a Dodger landmark, would be traded—he felt that it was one more example of unfair treatment from Walter O'Malley. "Even by baseball's chilly standards of conduct in such matters," Arnold Rampersad writes, "the trade seemed arctic."

Robinson, because of his agreement with *Look* magazine, did not respond to Bavasi—he kept quiet, which some thought was deceptive, about the news of his Chock Full o'Nuts contract. He received his "official release notice" from the Dodgers a few days later, and still he uttered not a word. When the article appeared in *Look* a few weeks later, the sports world—and the Dodgers and Giants—were rocked by the news. O'Malley and Bavasi were furious, charging that Robinson should have told them he planned to retire, although, as Rampersad points out, they made no point to tell him that they planned to trade him. Many fans felt betrayed, especially the Giants fans, who had thought for the past few weeks that Robinson would be in a

Jackie Robinson took a call in January 1957 in his new office at Chock Full o'Nuts in New York City. He had become the company's director of personnel. He accepted the position just as the Dodgers had agreed to trade him to the New York Giants.

Giants uniform the following season. Others fans and sportswriters, however, did not blame Robinson; they felt he had been a devoted ballplayer and that he deserved the enticement

that *Look* magazine had offered for his story. Anyone ,
shoes would have done the same thing.

So, between the 1956 and 1957 seasons, Jackie Rc
officially retired from baseball and joined a new team, t.
Chock Full o'Nuts.

THE NAACP

At this point in his life, Robinson also began what would
become a lifelong relationship with the National Association
for the Advancement of Colored People (NAACP). The oldest civil rights organization in the United States, the NAACP
had battled segregation for years, using the most prominent
African Americans and others as spokespeople for important causes.

It was an important time in the history of the African-
American community and of the nation as a whole. In 1954,
attorneys led by the dynamic Thurgood Marshall—who was
working for the NAACP—successfully overturned legalized
segregation in public schools in *Brown vs. the Board of
Education of Topeka, Kansas.* The NAACP had filed a lawsuit on
behalf of parents of students in Topeka, alleging that their children did not have the same access to a good public-school education as white students did. When the case finally reached the
United States Supreme Court, it combined four similar cases
from other states, all seeking the same resolution. The Supreme
Court unanimously found that racial segregation violated the
Fourteenth Amendment to the Constitution, which guarantees
citizens equal rights under the law. It also found that separate
facilities, by nature, are unequal.

The case blew open the race issue in the United States,
as it officially meant that African-American students could
not legally be kept out of white schools. Across the nation,
plans began to form to integrate school systems, but the back-
lash began just as quickly. The surge in the rate of violence

against African Americans was shocking—reported cases of lynchings increased dramatically as opponents of integration resorted to such methods to intimidate the black community. Threats were made against the NAACP, which was viewed as a leader in these cases: As Arnold Rampersad notes in his biography of Robinson, "Across the South, several school districts agreed to try to desegregate, but intransigence ruled in many more places. In Jack's native Georgia, for example, the board of education voted to revoke the license of any teacher who belonged to the NAACP or who taught a class made up of different races."

Robinson wanted to become involved in the fight to overturn segregation in the United States. In 1956, he was awarded the Spingarn Medal, the NAACP's highest honor, given to an African American whose success had lifted up his or her race. In accepting the medal, Robinson remarked in his speech that the NAACP's cause "is the cause of democracy, which makes it the champion of all Americans who cherish the principles on which this country was founded." Soon after, he agreed to become the national chairman of the NAACP's Fight for Freedom Fund campaign, which would take him on a tour of the nation to raise money for the organization. The campaign had started in 1953, with the goal of raising $1 million a year to help end segregation within 10 years. Robinson embraced the challenge with enthusiasm, and he turned out to be an excellent choice for the position.

He proved to be a polished, effective, and inspiring speaker. At one fundraising event in January 1957 in Oakland, California, he told a packed audience that the NAACP was working to gain the full rights, accorded to any citizen, for African Americans. He also told them that they had to support the organization's efforts in this endeavor: "If I had to choose between baseball's Hall of Fame and first-class citizenship, I would say first-class citizenship to all of my people." The speech inspired thunderous applause—the only time

★ ★ ★ ★ ★ ★

THE NAACP

The National Association for the Advancement of Colored People is one of the oldest civil rights organizations in the nation. It was founded in 1909 on February 12—the birthday of Abraham Lincoln—by a group of African Americans and whites, in reaction to the 1908 race riots that led to the deaths of many African Americans in Springfield, Illinois. The organization was an outgrowth of the Niagara Movement, an African-American group founded by W.E.B. DuBois in 1905, and it embarked on a nationwide campaign to educate others about racial inequality and to take progressive action.

In its early years, the NAACP worked to overturn Jim Crow laws through the court system. It organized opposition to President Woodrow Wilson's introduction of racial segregation into government policy, and the NAACP helped to win the right of African Americans to serve in World War I as officers. By 1920, the organization's membership had reached 90,000. Between the two world wars, the NAACP devoted much of its work to fighting the lynching of black people across the United States.

In 1954, the NAACP won a major battle when Thurgood Marshall, a lawyer with the organization, argued *Brown vs. the Board of Education of Topeka, Kansas* and won—the Supreme Court unanimously overturned segregation in public schools. It continued its work during the civil rights era and helped bring about civil rights legislation. In 1963, Medgar Evers, the NAACP field director in Mississippi, was assassinated in front of his home. Many other NAACP leaders received death threats or were victims of violence during this era.

The NAACP, which has its headquarters in Baltimore, Maryland, currently has a half-million members and continues to be active in the arena of civil rights.

people stopped clapping was when they were reaching for their wallets to make a donation.

POLITICALLY ACTIVE

Robinson traveled almost every week for the NAACP, appearing at fundraisers and meetings across the country. This hectic schedule, however, took a toll on his health and brought out a problem that had been quietly brewing for years: In 1957, he learned that, like two of his brothers, he was a diabetic. He worked with doctors to bring his condition under control, and he cut down on his commitments to some extent to allow himself time to relax and heal.

Robinson focused on politics during this time as well. He had always believed that working with white people was essential to improving the quality of life for African Americans. In his own experience, while he had the support of African-American fans who attended his games and cheered him on, it had been white people like Branch Rickey who had given him an opportunity in the first place. By being involved in politics, Robinson felt he could inspire change through white people with political power.

In 1960, he supported the presidential campaign of Richard Nixon, who was running against Senator John F. Kennedy of Massachusetts. Many people in Robinson's circle of friends, including his wife, Rachel, were surprised by his decision to support Nixon, but Robinson believed in the candidate and thought he would be the best person to help advance the cause of African-American rights. Nixon lost the election, however, and in ensuing years took actions that disappointed Robinson, who realized that his support had been ill-placed. (One of these actions occurred when Nixon refused to support Martin Luther King, Jr., who was jailed in Georgia in 1960; in another instance, Nixon chose Spiro Agnew, the governor of Maryland, who Robinson felt was unfriendly to

Presidential candidate Richard Nixon shook hands with Jackie Robinson in October 1960 during a campaign stop in Plainfield, New Jersey. At right was Nixon's wife, Pat. Robinson believed he could inspire change by working with people in prominent positions.

African-American issues, to be his running mate when he ran for president again in 1968.) In his memoir, Robinson wrote, "I do not consider my decision to back Richard Nixon over John F. Kennedy for the presidency in 1960 one of my finer ones. It was a sincere one, however, at the time. The Richard Nixon I met back in 1960 bore no resemblance to the Richard Nixon as president."

HALL OF FAME

Baseball players are eligible to be elected into the Baseball Hall of Fame five years after their retirement. In 1962, Jackie Robinson was technically eligible, but he doubted he would receive

☆ ☆ ☆ ☆ ☆ ☆

THE NATIONAL BASEBALL HALL OF FAME AND MUSEUM

The brick building in Cooperstown, New York, stands as the central point for the study and preservation of baseball history in the country and the world. Opened in 1939, the National Baseball Hall of Fame and Museum was originally founded by private investors who sought to restore Cooperstown's economy, which was ravaged by the Great Depression. They used the legend—doubted by some—that baseball was actually invented in Cooperstown as a public-relations launching point to generate media attention for the Hall of Fame.

The Hall of Fame began to acquire baseball memorabilia, including the uniforms and mitts of famous players, as well as media items, like newspaper clippings and photos. The process of inducting members into the Hall of Fame was established as well, to recognize those players who excelled during their ballplaying careers.

The museum currently welcomes 350,000 tourists a year, and it features exhibits and galleries, all to celebrate the history of the sport. It also has a research library, which collects and maintains archives of the history of the game. Some of the museum's most famous and most frequently visited sections include the Babe Ruth Room, the Hank Aaron Room, and the Plaque Room, which displays the plaques of those inducted into the Hall of Fame.

the honor. Rarely were players elected in the first year they were eligible; it usually took a few years. To be named to the Hall of Fame, a player has to receive 75 percent of the vote by the members of the Baseball Writers' Association of America.

Sportswriters across the country debated whether Robinson would receive the honor. One columnist, Dick Young of the New York *Daily News*, mused:

> He made enemies. He had a talent for it. He has the tact of a child because he had the moral purity of a child. When you are tactless, you make enemies. Perhaps "enemies" is a harsh word. I rather think Robinson displeased people and offended them. He made few friends among the newsmen. . . . On ability alone, a strong case can be made for Jackie Robinson: for his .311 batting average through a 10-year career with the Dodgers, for his ability to beat you with his bat, with his glove, with his waddling speed. Jackie Robinson made baseball history and that's what the Hall of Fame is, baseball history.

Within this passage, one can see the contradicting opinions that existed regarding Robinson's potential for election to the Hall of Fame.

The question was resolved on January 23, 1962, when he received a phone call telling him that he had earned just slightly more than the 75 percent of the ballots (124 of 160) needed to be elected. Robinson was overwhelmed: "Truthfully, after having steeled myself to be passed over and not to let it hurt me a lot, I was almost inarticulate."

Two of the first people he called were Branch Rickey and his mother, Mallie Robinson, both of whom flew in to attend his induction ceremony at the Hall of Fame in Cooperstown, New York. Robinson was proud to have them, as well as Rachel, by his side—the three people who had done the most to

Jackie Robinson held up his Hall of Fame plaque during induction ceremonies in 1962 at the National Baseball Hall of Fame and Museum in Cooperstown, New York. Robinson was elected to the Hall of Fame in his first year of eligibility.

support him as he sought to realize his dreams. During the ceremony, when he addressed the audience, he said that he owed his achievement to his wife, his mother, and Branch Rickey, and he asked them to come up to the stage and stand beside him to share his honor.

The plaque in the Hall of Fame reads:

JACK ROOSEVELT ROBINSON
BROOKLYN N.L. 1947 TO 1956
Leading N.L. batter in 1949. Holds fielding mark for second baseman playing in 150 or more games with .992. Led N.L. in stolen bases in 1947 and 1949. Most Valuable Player in 1949. Lifetime batting average .311. Joint record holder for most double plays by second baseman, 137 in 1951. Led second basemen in double plays 1949-50-51-52.

Also in January, Robinson accepted an offer from the *Amsterdam News*, a weekly African-American newspaper based in New York City, to write his own column. In the column, entitled "Jackie Robinson Says" (and later called "Home Plate"), he could share his musings on almost any topic he wanted. He had had a newspaper column in the past, writing for the *New York Post* as well as an African-American paper, the *Citizen-Call*, and he even had a radio program at one point as well. Those jobs, however, had sometimes ended on a sour note, as when the *Post* fired him, most likely for his support of Richard Nixon.

As it turned out, he was given more editorial freedom by the *Amsterdam News*, and he embraced it. The column became his sounding board on issues of business, civil rights, sports, and politics. In this way, he felt he could reach a wider and more varied audience.

Troubling Times

On September 15, 1963, a Sunday morning, the Ku Klux Klan bombed the Sixteenth Street Baptist Church in Birmingham, Alabama. The terrorist action killed four girls who were in the basement of the church, in the Sunday-school room—11-year-old Denise McNair and 14-year-olds Addie Mae Collins, Carole Robertson, and Cynthia Wesley. The attack wounded 20 other church members.

The bombing of the Sixteenth Street Baptist Church sparked fury across the nation and renewed calls for racial justice, equality, and an end to segregation and race-based violence. Dr. Martin Luther King, Jr., who had often spoken at meetings, vigils and other civil rights activities held at the church, delivered the eulogy at the funeral of the four young victims.

★ ★ ★ ★ ★ ☆

DR. MARTIN LUTHER KING, JR.

Dr. Martin Luther King, Jr., was born on January 15, 1929, in Atlanta, Georgia. His grandfather and father had been the pastors at Ebenezer Baptist Church in Atlanta, and Martin was thus destined to take over the pastorship as well. He attended public schools in Georgia, which were segregated because of Jim Crow laws. He earned a bachelor of arts degree from Morehead College in Atlanta, a bachelor of divinity degree from the Crozer Theological Seminary in Chester, Pennsylvania, and a doctorate degree from Boston University.

In 1954, Martin Luther King, Jr., became pastor of the Dexter Avenue Baptist Church in Montgomery, Alabama. In December 1955, he led the first major nonviolent protest of racial discrimination: the Montgomery bus boycott, sparked by Rosa Parks's refusal to give up her seat on a public bus to a white man. The boycott, which lasted more than a year, boosted King to national fame. He soon began to work on a major campaign of nonviolent protest, making him the pre-eminent African-American leader. He led many peaceful marches, boycotts, and protests, including the "March on Washington for Jobs and Freedom" in 1963. There, he gave his famous "I Have a Dream" speech. *Time* magazine named King the Man of the Year in 1963. The March on Washington and other actions helped bring about the passage of the Civil Rights Act of 1964.

Also in 1964, at the age of 35, he was awarded the Nobel Peace Prize for his civil rights work. King was the youngest recipient of the Peace Prize. His work continued in 1967, when he initiated a "Poor People's Campaign" to address economic inequities that had not been covered in earlier civil rights legislation.

Attending a civil rights rally in Birmingham, Alabama, in May 1963 were *(from right)* Jackie Robinson, Dr. Martin Luther King, Jr., the Reverend Ralph Abernathy, and boxer Floyd Patterson. The man at far left is unidentified. Robinson became quite active with Dr. King and his work with the Southern Christian Leadership Conference.

Dr. King had risen to prominence in 1955, when he was a young minister in Alabama. On December 1, 1955, Rosa Parks was on her way home after a hard day at work when she refused to give up her seat on a bus in Montgomery, Alabama, to a white man; she was arrested for her defiant act. Local leaders organized a major boycott of the Montgomery bus system—a significant number of its passengers were African American. The boycott effort, led mainly by Dr. King, crippled the bus system; the U.S. Supreme Court ruled that segregation on the bus system was unconstitutional. This victory was an important one in the civil rights movement, which established racial equality and the abolishment of segregation as its goal.

King was the leader of the Southern Christian Leadership Conference (SCLC), a faith-based organization that sought to win civil rights for African Americans and end segregation through nonviolent means. King was a hero to many, and an enemy to others, and Americans regarded him as the primary leader in the movement for racial equality.

Robinson had been a spokesman and figurehead with the NAACP, and as King's nonviolent movement gained momentum, he lent his support to the Southern Christian Leadership Conference.

When he was inducted into the Hall of Fame, Robinson donated the proceeds of the celebration dinner to the SCLC to help finance its voter-registration drive. In May 1963, a few months before the infamous bombing, Robinson attended a civil rights rally in Alabama at the request of King. In June 1964, also at King's request, he spoke at a rally in Florida, shortly before the Civil Rights Act of 1964 was approved.

A POLITICAL CAREER

In 1964, Jackie retired from Chock Full o'Nuts after seven years with the company. His work on behalf of the civil rights movement had often detracted from his ability to do his job well, but his boss, William Black, had always supported his endeavors. In 1964, however, Robinson had an opportunity that he did not want to pass up: Governor Nelson Rockefeller of New York asked him to be one of six deputy national directors of his campaign for the presidency.

Once again (as with his backing of Nixon), Robinson was one of very few African Americans supporting a Republican candidate. He viewed it, however, as an opportunity to make both major political parties court the black vote and, therefore, pay attention to black issues and black concerns. Nevertheless, the Republicans nominated Barry Goldwater, who Robinson felt was a bigot, to run for president, and Robinson became disillusioned with the Republican Party. However, he remained a close friend of Nelson Rockefeller, who he felt believed in change and was concerned about racism in the United States.

Goldwater, a senator from Arizona, tried to win Robinson's support for his own campaign, but Robinson refused to meet with him. Instead he wrote him a letter, which he released to the press. In part, his letter said:

> You say to me that you are interested in breaking bread with me and discussing your views on civil rights. Senator, on pain of appearing facetious, I must relate to you a rather well-known story regarding the noted musician, Louis Armstrong, who was once asked to explain jazz. "If you have to ask," Mr. Armstrong replied, "you wouldn't understand."

Robinson said in his memoir that "I admit that I think, live, and breathe black first and foremost." He did not want a political campaign to corrupt his views and values.

In 1966, Rockefeller appointed Robinson to be a member of his Executive Chamber as the special assistant to the governor for community affairs. In this new position, Robinson served as a close advisor to the governor and could have more of an impact on race issues in the state of New York.

Robinson also decided to make an impact on the African-American community in a different way. In early 1964, he and several colleagues established Freedom National Bank, a bank that would primarily work in the interests of the African-American community. One main issue facing the community was that, because of racism, black people often had problems acquiring loans to buy homes, establish businesses, and generally improve their lives financially. Freedom Bank was established to allow more people in the African-American community to secure the funding they needed to

Jackie Robinson and Branch Rickey are shown talking during the Chicago Baseball Writers Association annual dinner in 1948. In 1965, Rickey died at the age of 83, and Robinson felt as if he had lost his father. Robinson was upset to see few African-American baseball players at Rickey's funeral.

better their lives and improve their futures. Also the bank was a way for African Americans to become more integrated into the economy in general.

MR. RICKEY

In December 1965, Robinson received word that Branch Rickey had died at the age of 83. Robinson felt as if he had lost his own father. Indeed, he had never known his father, Jerry

Robinson, but Rickey's protectiveness over Jackie and support of his career had been fatherly. "Branch Rickey," he wrote, "especially after I was no longer in the sports spotlight, treated me like a son."

Robinson attended Rickey's funeral, and he was angered to see that very few African-American ballplayers were present. By the time of Rickey's death in 1965, African Americans in baseball were no longer a rare sight; they had been fully accepted into the professional leagues, while the Negro baseball leagues had faded away. The integration of professional baseball was completed, and that achievement had been hard-earned by Rickey, who had had the vision to imagine it and the personal strength to make it happen.

"I could not understand why some of the other black superstars who earn so much money in the game today had not even sent flowers or telegrams," Robinson wrote. He also reflected on the fact that, even though African Americans played baseball, very few were in the administrative end of the game—as managers, presidents, and owners of clubs. Only then would he consider professional baseball to be fully integrated.

"The day of the black manager is coming," he predicted, "but only because it is inevitable. It will get here when an owner finally realizes that the argument that white players will not accept advice and orders from a black is phony."

He added, "Baseball had better wake up. You can't keep taking all and giving practically nothing back."

Coming Home

On March 4, 1968, Jackie Robinson was sitting in his office in Manhattan when a newspaper reporter called to ask how he felt about the news that his son, Jackie Robinson, Jr., 21, had been arrested for possession of drugs and a gun. The news came as a complete shock to Jackie.

Jackie Robinson, Jr., had been a bright-eyed, happy child who sat on his mother's lap during baseball games to watch his father make history as he played. As the wives of the other Dodgers' players learned to accept Rachel, Jackie, Jr., became friends with other white children; when the Robinsons moved to Connecticut, Jackie's friends and classmates were mostly white. It was not until Sharon and David attended school that Jackie and Rachel understood that they needed to give Jackie,

Jr., exposure to other African-American children so that he did not always feel like he was different, the odd one out.

Jackie, Jr., grew to adolescence with a feeling of insecurity, and his grades in school suffered for it. Part of the problem was that he was the son of the famous Jackie Robinson, and he even carried his father's name, so he felt as if he was perpetually being compared with his celebrity dad and was failing to live up to his reputation. Sharon, his sister, later said, "Jackie was thrown into the Noble Experiment alongside our parents, and because of his name, there was no hiding place."

At one point, in 1963, on the day his father had come home after a hospital stay, Jackie, Jr., ran away with a friend to California. Deeply hurt, the elder Jackie Robinson sobbed like a child, more for the fact that he could not get through to his own son. Jackie, Jr., returned home after his plan to find work in California failed, but his relationship with his parents remained tense.

A year later, Jackie, Jr., joined the Army, which his parents hoped would provide him with a sense of discipline and responsibility. However, Jackie, Jr.'s unit was shipped out in 1965 to Vietnam, where a vicious war was raging and many Americans were being killed. Rather than help him, the military experience traumatized the younger Robinson, who had seen his friends gunned down in front of him and had himself been injured. Moreover, when he returned to the United States, he fell into a deep depression.

Until 1968, when Robinson received that phone call, the Robinsons had not known that their son's depression had led him to use drugs. According to Arnold Rampersad's description of the arrest, "Narcotics officers had broken up a drug sale in front of the Allison-Scott Hotel in downtown Stamford. Shots were fired both by the police and by Jackie, who fled the scene but was apprehended not far away, on South Street. He was now in the Stamford jail, held on $5,000 bail."

The arrest of Jackie Robinson's son made the news; in fact, his sister, Sharon, heard about it while sitting in her car listening to the radio. Rachel and Jackie Robinson went to the station to pick up their son and post his bail; reporters were waiting for them and snapped pictures and asked questions. Robinson, tired and upset, told a reporter, "I've had more effect on other people's kids than on my own," but then clarified his statement: "I couldn't have had an *important* effect on anybody's child, if this happened to my own."

The news of their son's drug use deeply upset Rachel and Jackie, who did not understand how they could not have seen this problem coming or known that their son was an addict. "When the roof caved in," Robinson later wrote, "when Jackie got into deep trouble, I realized that I had been so busy trying to help other youngsters that I had neglected my own."

Jackie Robinson, Jr., was given a choice of jail time or entering a drug-rehabilitation program. He entered a program selected by his mother, who had completed her nursing degree and knew some colleagues who had suggested a good place for Jackie, Jr.

A DEATH AND A RECOVERY

A month after the arrest of Jackie, Jr., the Robinsons—and the nation—were devastated by the news of the assassination of Dr. Martin Luther King, Jr., in Memphis, Tennessee. He had been in Memphis to support a strike by sanitation workers. A sniper gunned King down as he stood on the balcony of his hotel room.

The news shocked Robinson, who loved and respected the work and vision of King. "At the funeral services," he wrote, "I was plunged into deep contemplation as I thought of the sadness of saying farewell to a man who died still clinging to a dream of integration and peace and nonviolence."

The year continued to be a troubling one for Robinson. Jackie, Jr.'s rehabilitation program was not succeeding—

he was discharged, but he went back almost immediately to using drugs.

Finally, he enrolled in the Daytop program, a rehabilitation center in Seymour, Connecticut, that was founded and run by recovering drug addicts. Robinson wrote later that the Daytop program helped restore his son's respect for and love of life. "The Daytop philosophy states firmly that no one owes the addict a living," Robinson wrote. "He owes a lot to life. And the task of recovering is his alone."

By pushing Jackie, Jr., to the limits, by not allowing him to get away with lies or deceit, by forcing him to face up to the responsibility of how his addiction had hurt him and his family, the Daytop program succeeded in helping him to recover. Shortly after he was discharged, he decided to join Daytop as a staff member to help other addicts.

Jackie and Rachel Robinson held a picnic at their house for the Daytop staff to show their appreciation of what the program had done for their son. Following an afternoon of good food and fun, as Jackie, Jr., started to board the bus to return to Daytop, he gave his father a hug.

"That single moment paid for every bit of sacrifice, every bit of anguish, I had ever undergone. I had my son back," Robinson wrote.

". . . ONE OF THOSE STRONG BLACK WOMEN"

While Jackie, Jr., was in the Daytop program, Jackie and Rachel Robinson suddenly had to worry about their second child, Sharon, who had decided to marry her high school boyfriend. On April 27, 1968, she did so, though her parents were unsure about her decision. She was only 18 years old. They were correct—the marriage was troubled from the beginning and would end in divorce after one year.

On May 21, almost a month after Sharon's wedding, Mallie Robinson collapsed in front of her home in Pasadena, California. Robinson flew to Los Angeles to be with her, but she died before he was able to arrive. Robinson was devastated, but he knew his mother had been proud of him. She had invested her energy and devotion in him, and in return, he had become successful, and he had provided her with a comfortable living.

"Mallie Robinson," he said simply. "She had been one of those strong black women you always hear about, women who have been the very salvation of the black people."

He reflected on how, as a young man, he had always been upset when his mother generously gave to others, even when she could barely feed herself and her large family. He understood, however, that she had never let others take advantage of her: "She had not been a fool for others. She had given with her eyes as open as her heart. In death she was still teaching me how to live."

DEVASTATION

On June 17, 1971, Robinson was home with David and Sharon, who was waiting to be picked up early in the morning to attend a friend's graduation ceremony. Rachel Robinson was in Massachusetts at a conference.

Jackie, Jr., had been busy planning a fundraising event for the Daytop program, which was to be held in several days at the Robinsons' home in Connecticut. As he drove from New York City to his parents' home, his car spun out of control on the Merritt Parkway. The car crashed into the guardrail, and the impact broke Jackie, Jr.'s neck. He died quickly. He was 24 years old.

The police arrived at the Robinson home before dawn. Though the officer tried to break the news gently, Jackie, Sharon, and David knew that Jackie, Jr., was dead.

David went to the hospital to identify the body, while Sharon and Jackie drove to Massachusetts to tell Rachel before the media got to her. They broke the news to her and then drove home together. For several days, Rachel could not stop crying and Jackie, whose own health was faltering because

Jackie Robinson consoled his wife, Rachel, as they were leaving
Antioch Baptist Church in Brooklyn after funeral services for their son,
Jackie Robinson, Jr., who died in a car accident in June 1971. In the
foreground are David *(without beard)*, the Robinsons' other son, and
Sharon, their daughter.

of his diabetes, was also having difficulty coping. Sharon and David, themselves crushed by the loss of their brother, held the family together.

The Robinsons decided to hold the benefit fundraiser that Jackie, Jr., had planned. It had been his dream to hold a small jazz festival to raise money for Daytop, which had helped him take back his life and conquer his addiction. After all the hard work he had invested, his family did not want to cancel it. Expected to raise $15,000, the benefit actually raised more than $40,000 as more people than anticipated turned out to pay tribute not just to Daytop but also to Jackie Robinson, Jr.

The day was a difficult one for Robinson, but he bore the pain of it for the memory of Jackie, Jr.

COMING HOME

In June 1972, Jackie Robinson's number, 42, was retired by the Dodgers during a ceremony held at Dodger Stadium. Later that year, Major League Baseball asked Robinson to throw out the ceremonial first ball during a World Series game, to commemorate the twenty-fifth anniversary of his entry into the major leagues. He was happy to attend, and to speak his mind.

"I am extremely proud and pleased," he said, according to Rampersad's book. "I'm going to be tremendously more pleased and more proud when I look at that third-base coaching line one day and see a black face managing in baseball."

Less than two weeks later, on October 24, 1972, Jackie Robinson died of a heart attack. His diabetes had taken a toll on him in recent years, causing him to become nearly blind. The stress of his son's death had also been very difficult to bear.

His body lay in state at a funeral home, and after a service at Riverside Church in Harlem, he was buried on October 29 in Cypress Hills Cemetery in Brooklyn, where his son was also buried, only a few blocks from where Ebbets Field once stood.

Jackie Robinson's casket was carried from Riverside Church in Harlem after his funeral service in October, 1972. His pallbearers included Bill Russell *(left)*, the former Boston Celtics star, and Ralph Branca *(behind him)* and Don Newcombe *(right)*, both former Dodger pitchers.

During his eulogy at Robinson's funeral, the Reverend Jesse Jackson said, "Jackie as a figure in history was a rock in the water, creating concentric circles and ripples of new possibility."

Indeed, Jackie Robinson's legacy is that of setting a standard of excellence by which other African-American athletes—in any sport—would be judged. His performance, on and off the baseball diamond, allowed other white ballclub owners to take a chance on more African-American players and slowly, very slowly, the closed vault of American sports was opened.

Nevertheless, it is true that the "first" is always a lonely figure. Few sports fans and athletes today can appreciate or even imagine what it felt like to be Jackie Robinson in 1947—to be a man with tremendous talent, despised for the color of his skin. Author Cal Fussman wrote, "I grew up watching the great black ballplayers who followed in Jackie Robinson's footsteps,

☆ ☆ ☆ ☆ ☆ ☆

RETIRING NO. 42

"No. 42 belongs to Jackie Robinson for the ages."

Bud Selig, then the acting baseball commissioner, said those words on April 15, 1997, during a ceremony to mark the fiftieth anniversary of Jackie Robinson's first game with the Brooklyn Dodgers. On that day in 1997, Major League Baseball retired Robinson's number to honor the pioneering player.

"The day Jackie Robinson stepped on a major-league field will forever be remembered as baseball's proudest moment," Selig said at the ceremony, held during a game between the Los Angeles Dodgers and the New York Mets at Shea Stadium. "Major League Baseball is retiring No. 42 in tribute to his great achievements and for the significant contributions he made to society."

With the retirement of Robinson's number, no new players in the major leagues may use No. 42. Any players in 1997 who wore No. 42 were allowed to keep the number for the rest of their careers. The only player still active in 2007 with No. 42 is Mariano Rivera, the relief pitcher for the New York Yankees.

"The legacy that Jackie left for us, especially as a minority player like me, being the last one to wear No. 42 is an honor, and I do carry it with honor," Rivera said in an interview in 2007. "I'm blessed."

The Los Angeles Dodgers, with every player wearing No. 42, lined up during the singing of the National Anthem before a game on April 15, 2007—Jackie Robinson Day. More than 200 players and coaches donned Robinson's number that day to commemorate the sixtieth anniversary of his first game with the Brooklyn Dodgers.

but I didn't have a clue about what I was seeing because I had no idea what was going on inside their heads or their hearts, in their personal lives, or even on the field. I had no idea what real pressure was." He imagines how Robinson must have felt, day after day, getting up and walking onto the field to play before a hostile crowd, with teammates who resented him and players from other clubs who openly tried to hurt him. "By the end of that first season," Fussman writes, "Jackie had swallowed centuries of condensed pressure and performed above it."

Hank Aaron, an African-American ballplayer, who was one of the greatest players the sport has seen, commented in 1999, "Jackie's character was much more important than his batting average. . . . To this day, I don't know how he withstood the things he did without lashing back."

Robinson's remarkable life continued to be recognized after his death. In 1984, President Ronald Reagan posthumously awarded Robinson the Presidential Medal of Freedom, one of the two highest civilian awards in the United States. The other is the Congressional Gold Medal, given by Congress, and Robinson posthumously received that accolade in 2003.

Major League Baseball continued to honor Robinson, as well. In 1987—40 years after he first played in the major leagues—the Rookie of the Year Award was renamed the Jackie Robinson Award. Ten years later, his number—42—was retired by Major League Baseball.

As baseball was preparing to mark the sixtieth anniversary of Robinson's entry into the major leagues in 2007, Cincinnati Reds right fielder Ken Griffey, Jr., wanted to celebrate Robinson's legacy in a special way. He asked Bud Selig, the baseball commissioner, for permission to wear No. 42 on April 15. Selig backed Griffey's idea and encouraged other teams to have players wear Robinson's number.

On April 15, 2007, more than 200 players, managers, and coaches—including all the members of the Los Angeles Dodgers, the St. Louis Cardinals, the Houston Astros, the Philadelphia Phillies, the Milwaukee Brewers, and the Pittsburgh Pirates—wore No. 42.

"If it weren't for Jackie Robinson, I wouldn't be able to put on the uniform I'm wearing today," Griffey said. "He should be an inspiration not only to baseball players but to anyone who fights prejudice and hatred."

STATISTICS

JACKIE ROBINSON
Primary position: Second base
(Also 3B; 1B; OF)

Full name: Jack Roosevelt Robinson
Born: January 31, 1919, Cairo, Georgia
Died: October 24, 1972, Stamford,
Connecticut • Height: 5'11" •
Weight: 204 lbs. • Team: Brooklyn
Dodgers (1947–1956)

☆ ☆ ☆ ☆ ☆ ☆

YEAR	TEAM	G	AB	H	HR	RBI	BA
1947	BRO	151	590	175	12	48	.297
1948	BRO	147	574	170	12	85	.296
1949	BRO	156	593	203	16	124	.342
1950	BRO	144	518	170	14	81	.328
1951	BRO	153	548	185	19	88	.338
1952	BRO	149	510	157	19	75	.308
1953	BRO	136	484	159	12	95	.329
1954	BRO	124	386	120	15	59	.311
1955	BRO	105	317	81	8	36	.256
1956	BRO	117	357	98	10	43	.275
TOTAL		1,382	4,877	1,518	137	734	.311

Key: BRO = Brooklyn Dodgers; G = Games; AB = At-bats; H = Hits; HR = Home runs;
RBI = Runs batted in; BA = Batting average

CHRONOLOGY

1919   **January 31** Born near Cairo, Georgia.

1920   Moves with his mother and siblings to Pasadena, California.

1937   Enrolls at Pasadena Junior College.

1939   Enrolls at UCLA.

1941   Meets Rachel Isum at UCLA.

1942   Joins the U.S. Army.

1945   Plays baseball for the Kansas City Monarchs of the Negro Leagues; signs contract with Branch Rickey to play for the Brooklyn Dodgers franchise.

1946   **February 10** Marries Rachel Isum.

Debuts with the Montreal Royals, the Dodgers' farm team.

November 18 Son Jackie Robinson, Jr., is born.

1947   Debuts with the Brooklyn Dodgers, becoming the first African-American player in the major leagues (in the modern era); named Rookie of the Year.

1949   Testifies before the House Un-American Activities Committee (HUAC); plays in first All-Star Game; named Most Valuable Player in the National League.

1950   **January 13** Daughter Sharon Robinson is born.

The Jackie Robinson Story, starring Robinson as himself, debuts in movie theaters.

1952   **May 14** Son David Robinson is born.

1955   Dodgers win World Series against the New York Yankees, their archrivals.

1957   Retires from professional baseball and becomes a business executive with Chock Full o'Nuts; begins to serve the National Association for the Advancement of Colored People.

1962   Elected to the Baseball Hall of Fame.

1966   Named special assistant to Governor Nelson Rockefeller of New York.

1968   His mother, Mallie Robinson, dies.

1971   His eldest son, Jackie Robinson, Jr., dies in a car accident.

1972   Jackie Robinson's number, 42, is retired by the Dodgers.

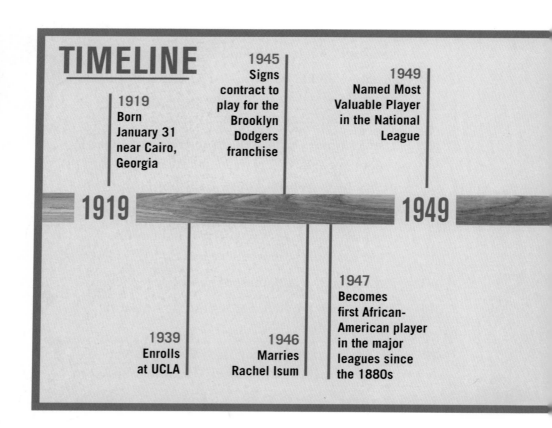

TIMELINE

1945 Signs contract to play for the Brooklyn Dodgers franchise

1919 Born January 31 near Cairo, Georgia

1949 Named Most Valuable Player in the National League

1919   1949

1939 Enrolls at UCLA

1946 Marries Rachel Isum

1947 Becomes first African-American player in the major leagues since the 1880s

October 24 Dies of a heart attack.

1984 Posthumously receives the Presidential Medal of Freedom.

1987 Major League Baseball renames the Rookie of the Year Award as the Jackie Robinson Award.

1997 Major League Baseball retires his number, 42.

2003 Posthumously receives the Congressional Gold Medal.

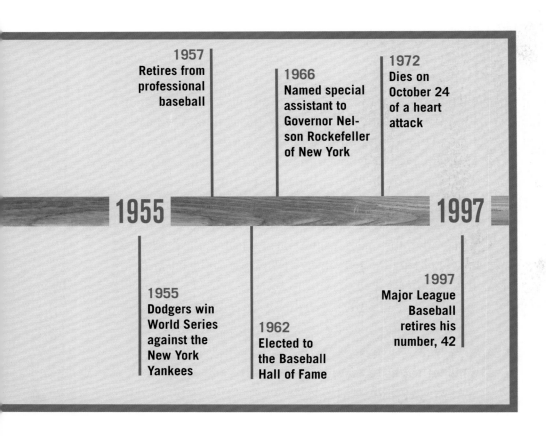

1957
Retires from professional baseball

1966
Named special assistant to Governor Nelson Rockefeller of New York

1972
Dies on October 24 of a heart attack

1955

1997

1955
Dodgers win World Series against the New York Yankees

1962
Elected to the Baseball Hall of Fame

1997
Major League Baseball retires his number, 42

GLOSSARY

at-bat   An official turn at batting that is charged to a baseball player, except when the player walks, sacrifices, is hit by a pitched ball, or is interfered with by a catcher. At-bats are used to calculate a player's batting average and slugging percentage.

barnstorming   A baseball tradition in which teams would assemble for a few months at a time, travel the region, and pick up baseball games wherever they could. Most players usually barnstormed in the off-season for extra money.

batting average   The number of hits a batter gets divided by the number of times the player is at bat. For example, 3 hits in 10 at-bats would be a .300 batting average.

bunt   A ball not fully hit, with the batter either intending to get to first base before the infielder can field the ball, or allowing an existing base runner to advance a base.

doubleheader   Two baseball games played by the same teams on the same day.

double play   A play by the defense during which two offensive players are put out in a continuous action. A typical combination is a ground ball to the shortstop, who throws to second base to get one runner out. The second baseman then throws to the first baseman to get the batter out.

dugout   The area where the players and managers not on the field can wait and watch. It usually has a bench with a roof, and in the major leagues includes a bat rack, glove and towel holders, a water cooler, a telephone to the bullpen, and more.

error   When a defensive player makes a mistake resulting in a runner reaching base or advancing a base, an error is designated by the game's scorer.

farm team   A team that provides training and experience for young players, with the expectation that successful players will move to the major leagues. The farm-team system was developed by Branch Rickey.

fielding percentage   A statistic that reflects the percentage of times a defensive player successfully handles a batted or thrown ball. It is calculated by the sum of putouts and assists divided by the number of total chances.

fungo   A fly ball hit so fielders may practice catching.

home run   When a batter hits a ball into the stands in fair territory, it is a home run. The batter may also hit an inside-the-park home run if the ball never leaves the playing field and the runner is able to reach home plate without stopping before being tagged by a defensive player. A home run counts as one run, and if there are any runners on base when a home run is hit, they score.

Jim Crow   The era, from 1876 to 1964, when segregation was enforced in the American South and other parts of the country.

pennant   The championship of each league in Major League Baseball.

runs batted in (RBI)   The number of runs that score as a direct result of a batter's hit(s) are the runs batted in by that batter. The major-league record is 191 RBIs for a single year by one batter.

sacrifice   A ball hit by the batter that advances a runner to the next base while the batter receives an "out" for his attempt. Examples include a sacrifice fly and a sacrifice bunt.

umpire   The official who rules on plays. For most baseball games, a home-plate umpire calls ball and strikes, and other umpires in the infield rule on outs at bases.

BIBLIOGRAPHY

Fussman, Cal. " 'After Jackie': A Definition of Pressure," ESPN.com. Available online at *http://sports.espn.go.com/mlb/jackie/news/story?id=2829674*

Holmes, Dan. "Remembering Jackie," National Baseball Hall of Fame and Museum. Available online at *http://www.baseballhalloffame.org/history/2005/050415.htm*

"Jackie Robinson Timeline," MLB.com. Available online at *http://mlb.mlb.com/NASApp/mlb/la/history/jackie_robinson_timeline/timeline_2.jsp*

Jackson, Jesse. "Jackie Robinson Eulogy," Baseball Almanac. Available online at *http://www.baseball-almanac.com/players/p_robij5.shtml*

Rampersad, Arnold. *Jackie Robinson: A Biography.* New York: Alfred A. Knopf, 1997.

Robinson, Jackie, with Alfred Duckett. *I Never Had It Made: An Autobiography of Jackie Robinson.* New York: Harper Perennial, 2003.

FURTHER READING

Eig, Jonathan. *Opening Day: The Story of Jackie Robinson's First Season.* New York: Simon & Schuster, 2007.

Fussman, Cal. *After Jackie: Pride, Prejudice, and Baseball's Forgotten Heroes.* New York: ESPN Books, 2007.

Hogan, Lawrence D. *Shades of Glory: The Negro Leagues and the Story of African-American Baseball.* Washington D.C.: National Geographic, 2006.

Lamb, Chris. *Blackout: The Untold Story of Jackie Robinson's First Spring Training.* Lincoln, Neb.: University of Nebraska Press, 2004.

Parrott, Harold. *The Lords of Baseball.* Atlanta: Longstreet Press, 2001.

Pollock, Alan J. *Barnstorming to Heaven: Syd Pollock and His Great Black Teams.* Edited by James A. Riley. Tuscaloosa, Ala.: The University of Alabama Press, 2006.

Robinson, Rachel. *Jackie Robinson: An Intimate Portrait.* New York: Abradale and Abrams, 1998.

Robinson, Sharon. *Promises to Keep: How Jackie Robinson Changed America.* New York: Scholastic, 2004.

WEB SITES

Baseball Almanac

http://www.baseball-almanac.com

Baseball Reference

http://www.baseball-reference.com

ESPN.com: "Jackie Changed Face of Sports"

http://espn.go.com/sportscentury/features/00016431.html

The Jackie Robinson Foundation

http://www.jackierobinson.org/

National Archives and Records Administration: Jackie Robinson Letter

http://www.archives.gov/exhibits/featured_documents/jackie_ robinson_letter/

National Baseball Hall of Fame and Museum

http://www.baseballhalloffame.org

The Official Site of Jackie Robinson

http://www.jackierobinson.com

The Time 100: Jackie Robinson

http://www.time.com/time/time100/heroes/profile/robinson01.html

PICTURE CREDITS

INDEX

Aaron, Hank, 86, 107
African Americans
  and communism, 59–64
  first in Major League Baseball,
    34, 36, 42, 45
  lynching, 82, 83
  media, 42, 89
  in the military, 23–26, 83
  and obstacles caused by racism,
    2, 6, 8, 12–15, 17–21, 23, 24,
    26, 28, 30–34, 36, 39–41, 43,
    46–50, 51, 57–59, 62, 66–67,
    70–71, 81, 82, 84–85,
    90–93, 94
  and poverty, 66–67
  race riots, 11, 83
  racial slurs against, 4, 14, 36, 41,
    47, 50, 64
Agnew, Spiro, 84–85
Alexander, Ted, 27
All-Star Games
  years in, 43, 59, 74
American Civil War, 7, 9
American League, 59
Amorós, Sandy, 75
Amsterdam News (newspaper),
  89
Armstrong, Louis, 94
Atlanta Braves, 43
Atlanta, Georgia
  racism in, 58–59

Baldwin, James, 60
Bankhead, Dan, 43
Bartlett, Ray
  childhood friend, 2, 4, 16
baseball
  commissioners, 31, 71, 73, 105,
    107
  fans, 36, 41, 45–46, 53, 55, 59, 65,
    71, 75, 79–80, 84, 106
  racism in, 9, 23, 28, 30–34, 36,
    39–41, 46–50, 57, 70, 96
  scouts, 31, 34

stealing bases, 18, 41, 53, 65, 75,
  89
  strike threat, 48–50
batting
  averages, 41, 43, 57, 65, 73–74,
    77, 87, 89, 107
  titles, 41, 43, 65
Bavasi, Buzzie, 79
Berra, Yogi, 75
Black, William
  and Chock Full o'Nuts, 78–79,
    93
Boston Braves
  games against, 45
Boston Red Sox, 30–31
Brooklyn, Dodgers
  contracts with, 36–37, 42, 54,
    58, 69
  fans, 45, 53, 55, 65, 75, 79–80
  farm team, 34, 37, 38–39, 41
  first game with, 45–46
  history of, 76
  and Jackie Robinson Day, 53
  management and coaches, 31,
    33–36, 42, 45, 47, 54, 57–58,
    70, 73, 76, 79
  move to Los Angeles, 76
  rookie of the year, 43, 53
  spring training, 42, 57, 58–59
  teammates, 42–48, 50, 54, 58, 75,
    97, 106
  and the World Series, 43, 54, 65,
    75–77
Brown v. the Board of Education of
  Topeka, 81, 83

Cairo, Georgia, 7, 8
Campanella, Roy, 43, 57–58
Chapman, Ben, 46–48
Chicago Cubs, 65
Chock Full o'Nuts coffee company
  work for, 78–79, 81, 93
Cincinnati Reds, 107
Civil Rights Act (1964), 91, 93

Civil rights movement, 9
    leaders, 81–84, 89, 90–94
Clemente, Roberto, 33
Cleveland Indians, 43
Collins, Addie Mae, 90
Congressional Gold Medal, 107
Cuban Giants, 28

Daytop rehabilitation program,
    100–101, 103
Dee, Ruby, 69
DiMaggio, Joe, 54
Downs, Karl, 37, 53
    death, 54–55
    influence on Jackie, 20–21, 23,
        27–28
Du Bois, W.E.B., 83
Durocher, Leo, 45

Ebbets, Charles, 76
Edwards, Bruce, 43
Evers, Medgar, 83

Foster, Rube, 28
Freedom National Bank, 94–95
Frick, Ford, 48–50, 71, 73
Fussman, Cal, 105–106

Gibson, Josh, 28
Goldwater, Barry, 94
Great Depression, 86
Griffey, Ken, Jr., 107

Hopper, Clay, 39
Horrell, Edwin "Babe," 6
House Un-American Activities
    Committee (HUAC), 59–64
Houston Astros, 107

Jackie Robinson Award, 107
Jackie Robinson: My Own Story, 55
Jackie Robinson Story, The (movie),
    67–69
Jackson, Jesse, 104

Kansas City Monarchs, 27
    playing for, 28, 30, 34
    teammates, 30
Kennedy, John F., 84–85
King, Martin Luther, Jr.
    assassination, 99
    and civil rights, 84, 90–93
Ku Klux Klan, 58, 60, 90

Landis, Kenesaw Mountain, 31
Lincoln, Abraham, 7, 31, 33, 83
Los Angeles Dodgers, 76, 103, 105,
    107
Louis, Joe, 25
Lucas, Bill, 43

Mann, Arthur, 68
March on Washington, 91
Marshall, Thurgood, 81, 83
McNair, Denise, 90
military, 62, 83
    in the army, 23–26, 27, 64
    discrimination in, 23–26
Milwaukee Brewers, 107
Montgomery, Alabama
    bus boycott, 91–92
Montreal Royals, 34
    contract with, 33, 36–37, 42
    manager, 39
    playing for, 38–41
    spring training, 38–39
    teammates, 39, 41
Musial, Stan, 65

National Association for the
    Advancement of Colored People
    (NAACP)
    Fight for Freedom Fund, 82
    history of, 83
    Spingarn Medal, 82
    work for, 81–82, 84, 93
National Baseball Hall of Fame, 82,
    86
    inductees, 33, 86–89, 93

National League, 48, 50, 59
  MVP, 43, 65, 69, 89
  pennant race, 53–54, 65, 74
Negro Leagues, 34, 42
  barnstorming, 57–58
  demise, 96
  fans, 30
  history of, 28
  teams in, 27–28, 30, 58
  travel, 30
Newcombe, Don, 43
New York Giants, 79–80
  games against, 46
New York Mets, 105
New York Yankees, 71, 105
  games against, 54, 75
  and the World Series, 54, 65, 75,
    77
Niagara Movement, 83
Nixon, Richard
  backing of, 84–85, 89, 93

O'Malley, Walter
  and the Dodgers, 70, 73, 76, 79
Ostermueller, Fritz, 53
Owens, Jesse, 3, 17

Paige, Satchel, 28
Parks, Rosa, 91, 92
Pasadena, California
  community, 6, 13
  family in, 12, 14–16
  racism in, 4, 6, 12–15, 20
  sports in, 15
Pasadena Junior College
  sports at, 1, 3, 17–19, 21
Pasadena Robinson Memorial, 3
Philadelphia Phillies, 107
  games against, 46–48
Pittsburgh Pirates, 33, 107
  games against, 53
Presidential Medal of Freedom, 107

Rampersad, Arnold,
  biography of Robinson, 3, 8, 18,
    31, 41, 50, 77, 79, 82, 98, 103

Reagan, Ronald, 107
Reese, Pee Wee
  Dodger teammate, 45, 75
Rickey, Wesley Branch, 32–33, 51, 68
  and the Brooklyn Dodgers, 31,
    33, 34–37, 42, 45, 54, 58, 70
  death, 33, 95–96
  fight against racism, 31–33
  help to Robinson, 35–36, 39, 45,
    68, 70, 84, 87–88, 96
  "Noble Experiment," 33, 34, 36,
    41, 47, 51, 98
Rivera, Mariano, 105
Robertson, Carole, 90
Robeson, Paul, 60–62, 64
Robinson, David (son), 71, 97, 101,
  103
Robinson, Edgar (brother), 8
Robinson, Frank (brother), 8
  death, 2, 4, 21, 55
  influence on Jackie, 3–4, 18
Robinson, Frank, 43
Robinson, Jackie
  arrests, 4, 6, 20, 26
  awards and honors, 43, 53, 65, 82,
    86–89, 107
  birth, 10
  charities, 55–56, 66–67
  childhood, 4, 11–12, 14–16
  chronology and timeline, 109–
    111
  death, 43, 103–104
  education, 1–2, 14, 15–16, 17, 21
  endorsements, 55
  faith, 20–21, 55, 64
  fame, 54, 55, 57, 66–67
  fighting spirit, 15–16, 70
  injuries and illnesses, 57, 73, 84,
    103
  and politics, 84–85, 93–94
  retirement, 79, 81, 86
  speed, 2, 18, 87
  statistics, 108
Robinson, Jackie, Jr. (son)
  arrest, 97–99
  childhood, 42, 45, 51, 69, 98

death, 101, 103
depression and drug abuse,
    98–100, 103
Robinson, Jerry (father), 95–96
    abandonment of family, 10–11
    sharecropper status, 8, 10–11
Robinson, Mack (brother), 8
    death, 3
    and the Olympics, 3, 17
    and sports, 3, 17, 18
Robinson, Mallie McGriff (mother),
    2, 53
    death, 100–101
    and education, 8, 16, 23
    family, 8, 10–12
    influence on, Jackie, 12, 14, 16,
        87–88
    work, 12, 14, 20
Robinson, Rachel Isum (wife), 62,
    84
    family, 42, 45, 51, 66, 71, 97,
        99–101
    marriage, 27, 35, 37
    moves, 38, 58, 71
    and racism, 39, 67, 71
    support to Jackie, 21, 23, 64, 69,
        73, 87–88
Robinson, Sharon (daughter), 99,
    101, 103
    childhood, 66, 69, 97–98
    marriage, 100
Robinson, Willa Mae (sister),
    8, 10
    care of Jackie, 14
Rockefeller, Nelson, 93–94
Roosevelt, Teddy, 10
Ruth, Babe, 46, 86

Samuel Houston College,
    27, 28
Sasser, James Madison, 8, 10–11
segregation
    in baseball, 9, 23, 28, 30–31, 33,
        34, 38–39, 42, 53, 58, 62, 96
    efforts to fight, 81–83, 90, 92–93
    hospitals, 9, 54–55

and Jim Crow laws, 7, 9, 17, 25,
    38, 54–55, 58, 62, 65, 83, 91,
    92–93
in the military, 23–26
in schools, 1–2, 9, 67, 81–83, 91
in the South, 7, 9, 11, 38–39, 58,
    82
Selig, Bud, 105, 107
Slaughter, Enos, 50, 65
slavery, 59
    emancipation of, 7, 9
    owners, 8
Southern Christian Leadership Con-
    ference, 93
Stanford University
    and black students, 1–2, 21
Stanky, Ed, 47
St. Louis Browns, 32
St. Louis Cardinals, 32–33, 65, 107
    games against, 48, 50

Thomas, Charles, 32–33
Time, 53

University of California, Los Angeles
    (UCLA)
    admission to, 1, 21
    fans, 6
    football at, 6
    sports at, 21
University of Southern California
    (USC), 1
    and black students, 2

Vietnam War, 98

Wesley, Cynthia, 90
Wilson, Woodrow, 83
Wood, John S., 59, 62
World Series, 32, 103
    championships, 43, 54, 65, 75–77
World War I, 83
World War II, 23, 24, 60, 66
Wright, Richard, 60

Young, Dick, 87

ABOUT THE AUTHOR

SUSAN MUADDI DARRAJ is associate professor of English at Harford Community College in Bel Air, Maryland. She is the senior editor of *The Baltimore Review* and the author of *The Inheritance of Exile*, a collection of short stories, published by University of Notre Dame Press.